Dream Talk

Could God Be Talking to You Through Your Dreams?

A balanced biblical and scientific
approach to the frequently misunderstood
subject of dreams

Katrina J. Wilson

NELSON BOOKS
A Division of Thomas Nelson Publishers
Since 1798

www.thomasnelson.com

DREAM TALK

Published in Nashville, Tennessee, by Thomas Nelson, Inc. www.thomasnelson.com

Nelson Books titles may be purchased in bulk for educational, business, fund-raising, or sales promotional use. For information, please e-mail SpecialMarkets@ThomasNelson.com.

Unless otherwise noted, all Scripture quotations are from the King James Version of the Bible. Scripture quotations marked AMP are from the Amplified Version of the Bible, Old Testament copyright © 1965, 1987 by the Zondervan Corporation, New Testament copyright © 1954, 1958, 1987 by the Lockman Foundation.

Passages added to the Amplified version by the translators are indicated by parentheses ( ). Additional explanations supplied by the author are indicated by brackets [ ].

Library of Congress Cataloging-in-Publication Data

Wilson, Katrina J.
  Dream talk : could God be talking to you through your dreams? : a balanced biblical and scientific approach to the frequently misunderstood subject of dreams / Katrina J. Wilson.
      p. cm.
  ISBN-13: 978-1-59951-032-3
  1. Dreams—Religious aspects—Christianity. I. Title.
  BR115.D74W55 2007
  248.2'9--dc22

                                        2006035178

Printed in the United States of America

1 2 3 4 5 6 — 10 09 08 07

Acknowledgments

My deepest appreciation is for my husband, Fred, for encouraging me to finish this book, which had been in my heart for years. Thank you, Rachel, my daughter, adviser, and manuscript typist. You cheerfully gave your time to decipher my handwritten notes. I also appreciate Jackie Mounts, a friend and member of our church, who sent me notes such as "Is the book finished yet? God." And to my dear friends at Christ Life Sanctuary and all of you who have heard this teaching on dreams, thank you. It was your confidence in me that gave me the courage to write this book that I hope will help others better understand the importance and impact of dreams and visions.

Last, but not in any way least, I want to thank my Lord, who sparked my desire to begin this study. May You, Oh Lord, receive the glory!

Contents

Contents

Foreword

John Mason

What really matters in life is what happens in us, not what happens to us. Do we change? Do we grow? Do we improve? We can get far by asking the right questions. In this book, *Dream Talk,* Katrina Wilson examines what happens in us while we sleep. And she answers the question "Is God speaking to us through our dreams?"

She explains that God speaks to us at night when we are still and silent, when we are more receptive to Him. While we dream, we can work through our frustrations and receive divine help. We can actually improve as a result of what we have learned in our dreams.

I've known Katrina for years. Her life and ministry are powerfully impacting people. Her knowledge of dreams comes from years of intense study of both the Bible and scientific works. She takes a balanced approach to the controversial subject of dream interpretation, and I believe her passion for teaching on this subject comes from a desire to see people follow God and go to the next level.

Introduction

It may seem strange that a pastor's wife would write a book on dreams. Actually, years ago, getting into a study like this would have been the farthest thing from my mind. I didn't know anyone who had ever taught on this subject. I had never read any books about dreams because, as far as I was concerned, dreams were not relevant for me as a person in the ministry. In fact, I had never thought that dreams were important for anyone.

However, I believe that God-ordained circumstances, which I'll explain later, brought the importance of dreams to my attention in such a way that I couldn't get away from it. I have always been a night owl and used to feel sleep was a waste of time. Because I taught from and studied the Bible for years, I knew the verse that says it was expedient for Jesus to go away so that the Holy Spirit Comforter could come to be with us always, but I didn't think "always" included sleep (John 14:16).

For some reason, I thought the Holy Spirit could only minister to me when I was awake. It may sound humorous, but I guess I thought that while I was asleep at night, the Holy Spirit went to the other side of the world to minister to those folks who were awake.

Years of studying both scriptural and scientific facts have given me a more balanced view of dreams, and I have been pleased to discover that the Bible and science do agree on the importance of dreams. Dreams are not New Age philosophy, even though some teach them as such. Dreams are not just a good idea but a God idea. Through testing, scientists have discovered that dreaming is absolutely necessary for a person's good health and sanity, but these are fairly recent ideas in the scientific community. For example, it was not until the 1950s that scientists began to have a breakthrough when they set up sleep labs to study the effects of the dreaming process in both adults and children.[1] The 1950s! However, much of the same information was recorded in the Bible thousands of years ago. It took a while but science finally has come into agreement with the Bible. Now that's good news!

Yet many of us still have not taken our dreams seriously. I've come to understand that this is partially because our Western tradition and culture have placed little importance on dreams, and it's easy for us to believe whatever our society promotes. Even though the Bible frequently mentions the powerful effects of dreams, I have been amazed to realize that there has been so little biblical teaching on the subject. Again, I believe this lack of teaching is due to the influence of our culture. People laughingly say (and I've done it myself), "I had the craziest dream last night," never realizing the importance of that dream. Many Christians believe that any teaching on dreams is just New Age thinking, and they stay away from it. After I teach on this subject, people often come to me, saying they never realized the Bible had anything to say about dreams. They had read the Bible for years, but due to their lack of knowledge, they just skipped over the verses about dreams. I did it for years, too! I believe this common situation is about to change.

It was fascinating to me when I discovered that approximately one-third of the Bible is related to dreams. There are not only thirty-four specific dreams recorded in the Bible—twenty-two in the Old Testament and twelve in the New Testament—but many more verses that share the importance and purpose of dreams, visions, and the night. Many people fear the night and are even afraid to go to sleep because they don't know what's out there. I believe the Bible makes us aware of dreams and their purpose in order to relieve that fear.

Let's look at the importance of dreams this way. There are twenty-four hours in a day, and we are supposed to sleep eight of those twenty-four hours. That means one-third of our life is spent in sleep. Either sleep is a waste of our valuable time, or it has purpose. Can sleeping be only to rest the body? Because one-third of our life is spent in sleep, it seems logical that this is an ideal time for us to get in touch with our true inner-self and also a time when God can communicate with us through the dreaming process at a time when there is no outside interference. I believe that by reading this book you will discover that this is one of the true purposes of sleep. Understanding this has caused my study on dreams to be an exciting personal journey.

Now let me share with you those God-given circumstances that catapulted me into this study.

Why Me, Lord?

When I look back on how I got into the study of dreams, I have to believe the verse that says that the steps of a good person are ordered by the Lord (Psalm 37:23). It was the fall of 1985, and we were in special church services. The speaker was the evangelist Rev. Dick Mills, known for his prophetic ministry. I sat in one of the services, being a dutiful pastor's wife and listening to the Rev. Mills, when suddenly I heard him call my husband and me to the front of the church. I was definitely in for a shock that night. We stood before a man who I considered a genuine man of God, when all at once I heard him say publicly, "The Lord is going to begin to speak to you through dreams and visions, and He will give you understanding. You will travel and teach others on this subject."

I was so stunned that I almost laughed out loud. My mind whirled. God will speak to me in dreams? And visions? I felt I had experienced a few visions, but they weren't something I talked about. How could this be from the Lord? I thought that surely this man had missed it.

Being in church most of my life, I have heard people share their dreams or visions. Some were good, of course, but others were what I considered somewhat *flaky,* if you know what I mean. Some of these people were also rather unstable in their lifestyle. Yet here was Rev. Mills telling me that I was going to be joining that group. I shuddered at the thought. That night, however, was the beginning of a life-changing study on the purpose of dreams and visions. I now realize that because people go overboard on a subject does not mean the subject itself is not genuine. Of course, I wasn't thinking that at the time. Believe me, I was definitely not a happy camper, and, at first, I did not take that shocking message to heart. I laid it on the shelf. If God wanted to speak to me in dreams and visions, He would have to bring it to pass. Weeks went by, and I didn't remember any of my dreams and wasn't having any visions. I felt justified that I had ignored Rev. Mills, and, honestly, I just forgot about it.

God did not.

Several months went by and, of course, I wasn't thinking about the subject of dreams. Then my husband, Fred, started having such vivid dreams that some of them woke him up in the middle of the night. These dreams seemed to occur about twice a week, and he would wake me up to tell me about his dreams. He had never done that before. There were occasions when we would end up in heated discussions, and I reminded him that I did not know anything about dreams and told him to interpret his own dreams. I think I felt just a little guilty and frustrated; after all, Rev. Mills' message had been to both of us. But Fred didn't quit. Every time he would remember a dream—it didn't matter what time it was—he would tell me about it. Then something started happening that really shook me. After a while, some of these dreams started coming to pass, as if the dreams were showing future events, things we had no way of knowing beforehand. That really caught my attention, but I still did not make any move to study dreams.

During this time, as Fred and I tried to work through his dream interpretations, I was teaching a Wednesday night class at our church. I announced one night that I was going to be sharing about Joseph and that the title of my message was "Don't Let Anyone Steal Your God-given Dreams." After that announcement, several people who remembered Rev. Mills and his word to Fred and me approached and said how glad they were that I was going to be obedient and teach on dreams. It was nice that they remembered, but I had only meant that we shouldn't let anyone steal our God-given *goals*. I panicked.

But the Lord didn't leave me in a state of panic; He is faithful. One of the ladies in our church gave me a book about dreams that had been written by a former pastor. This was the first time I had ever read anything on dreams, and the book gave me some good insight, but something near the end of his book concerned me greatly. The pastor shared that he had been asked to leave his denomination because of this teaching. Now that was discouraging! However, using my faith, I did use some of his teaching in my message and thought that would be the end of it. I had been obedient, though only partially. Again, I put the word about dreams back on the shelf. I didn't realize that the Lord was not finished with me. In fact, now I began to remember some of my dreams. A reverse took place, and I started waking Fred up in the middle of the night to tell him about my dreams.

Finally, through the Holy Spirit's continual prompting, I decided to try to study on this subject. I didn't even know where to begin, and I went to the public library. The librarian recommended a book, but it was not helpful. In fact, it was confusing. Then I went to several Christian bookstores, and all I got from the clerks were strange looks. In frustration and desperation, I finally prayed, giving my excuses to the Lord: "I have tried to study about dreams, but I can't find any books."

It was as if the Lord chuckled at me and said, "What is wrong with My Book?" "Your Book, Lord?" I responded. "You mean there is something in Your Book about dreams and visions?"

Thus began my wonderful journey as I studied from Genesis to Revelation every verse I could find about dreams, visions, and the purpose of the night. As I continued my research, I began to discover scientific studies that gave me great insight also. The result is this book, which is an in-depth study of biblical dreams and a comparison to the scientific view. I deal primarily with dreams and also include information on visions. Because dreams and visions are closely related, I want to give you a glimpse into both.

My goal is to help you, the reader, discover the impact that dreams can have on your life. After all, if you can dream it, you can do it. I also hope that you receive greater understanding about the purpose of visions and the importance of the night. After all, God created the night and said it was good (Genesis 1:18).

Chapter 1

Refreshing Dreams

When you lie down, you shall not be afraid; yes,
you shall lie down, and your sleep shall be sweet.

Proverbs 3:24 (AMP)

I can still see myself flying near the ceiling and looking down at my family. I sensed such exhilaration while flying from place to place. Oh, those were wonderful childhood dreams of flight! I actually looked forward to falling asleep at night so I could take another journey. I didn't know why I awoke with such a sense of relief after one of those dreams; I just knew I enjoyed it. Now I realize that flying is a symbolic dream that usually reveals the need to rise above difficult circumstances or to escape real life, and I understand why I so frequently dreamed of flying. At that time my parents were going through a divorce, and I was having a hard time coping when I was awake. But God gave me dreams to allow me times of escape.

Certainly, I'm not the only one who has had frequent dreams of flying. You probably have experienced them too. Recently, an evangelist asked me if I could help her understand her repeated childhood dreams. Because those dreams had lingered with her so long, she had even gone to a psychologist to get some understanding, and he could not help her. I smiled as she began to share with me her childhood dreams of *flying*. As soon as I mentioned the meaning of flying in a dream, she began to laugh and cry at the same time. She immediately sensed relief and peace. Although she grew up in an abusive home, she now understands how God's mercy allowed her through her journeys of flight to rise above those terrible times in her adolescent life.

Flying in a dream is not just for children. One day as I was watching television, a minister shared his recent dream—a dream of flying—with the host of the program. Although the minister was laughing as he told his seemingly "silly" dream, I could sense his inner struggle. I leaned over and told Fred that I wished I could help this man understand his dream. Of course, I thought I'd never see him, so I just let it go. However, a few months later he came to our church as a guest speaker. He had heard that I taught about dreams, and he told me about his recent flying dreams. As I shared the symbolic meaning, tears welled up in his eyes. He told me how he had been crying out to the Lord for help because he had been under tremendous stress. He said, "I didn't realize the Lord had heard me and was answering me even as I slept."

You see, sometimes we find ourselves in circumstances that we just do not know how to handle, or we get too busy when we're awake to listen to God. But I have discovered that during those times of stress, we can get some of the help and wisdom we need through our dreams.

Sleep-Deprived People

Before I even get into this study about dreams, I want to emphasize that sleeping and dreaming go together. If you don't sleep, you won't dream. If you think that sleep is just a time for your body to get some rest, you'll be just as I was, and you won't care if you get the proper sleep. In fact, it seems many Americans have difficulty getting enough sleep.

I have read several articles written by doctors who are concerned about Americans' sleeping habits. One study, conducted by the National Sleep Foundation in 2001, revealed that more than forty percent have sleep disorders such as insomnia and heavy snoring, and 50 percent claim lack of sleep as a major problem. Dr. William C. Dement, director of a sleep clinic at Stanford University School of Medicine, said, "There is no doubt that sleepy drivers kill people all the time." In the United States, drowsy drivers cause at least 100,000 automobile crashes each year, according to the National Highway Traffic Safety Administration.[2]

At the time of this writing, the most recent study (conducted in 2001 by the National Sleep Foundation) discovered that 48 percent of eighteen- to twenty-nine-year-olds and 28 percent of thirty- to sixty-five-year-olds have no regular sleep patterns, and this lack of sleep is taking a toll on the health and emotions of both adults and children. Scientists attribute this to the complexity of modern life. Doctors say that most people watch TV or listen to the radio before going to sleep, and this is not a relaxing way to fall asleep. Teachers are complaining that too many children are coming to school so sleepy that they have difficulty learning. These children are following their parents' sleep habits.

To further emphasize this fact, Thomas Roth, head of the division of sleep medicine at Henry Ford Hospital in Detroit, Michigan, has found that insomnia, a sign of anxiety or ill health, is the complaint of half of the American population. He found that getting too little sleep is affecting people's memory and mood.[3] These findings are frightening.

Scientists tell us that adequate sleep, on the other hand, makes people more alert and productive. Even though most of us no doubt know this, it seems we still allow the pressures of life to mold us into a poor sleep pattern. Scientists are alarmed that not getting enough sleep is becoming a national epidemic. Be assured, however, that you do not have to be a sleep-deprived American!

Why am I emphasizing your need for sleep? Because it is during your time of sleep that you go through the stages of sleep and dreaming. It takes an extended time of uninterrupted sleep to go through these stages. Experts have proved through testing conducted in sleep labs that these stages of sleep and dreaming are absolutely necessary for people to have physical and emotional balance during their waking hours. When you do not get enough sleep, you do not go through these sleep cycles. You may awake tired, stiff, and groggy, with a fuzzy mind and usually in a bad mood.[4]

When I read these reports, I realized these experts were proving that through sleep and through the dreams during our sleep we receive the refreshing we need. If you struggle over going to sleep, pray before going to bed and commit your time of sleep and your dreams to the Lord.

I know that, for the most part, you are not thinking about your sleep and dream patterns. In fact, they have probably never been thoughts in your mind, but I believe that when you begin to understand the purpose of sleep and dreaming, you will look forward to your time of "sweet sleep," as Proverbs 3:24 calls it. The Hebrew meaning of "sweet" is "secure, pleasant, a time of divine exchange, to intertwine and braid together." There has been a divine plan put in place, and it's good to know that you are not without hope during the day or in the night. When you lie down to sleep at night, you do not have to be afraid. You can know your sleep will be sweet!

20

Was It a Dream or a Vision?

I the LORD will make myself known unto him in a vision, and will speak unto him in a dream.

Numbers 12:6

According to dream experts, a dream is a series of symbolic pictures (images and ideas) that surface in your mind during sleep. These meaningful and sometimes spiritual messages come every night whether you remember your dreams or not.[5]

In the Bible, one of the biblical Hebrew meanings for dreams is *chalam,* which refers to something seen in sleep and means to cause to dream or to bind firmly upon the heart that which is seen in sleep. You may think that most of your dreams are not bound to your heart and, in fact, are easily forgotten or never remembered. You may feel that even when you remember a dream it seems disjointed or jumps from scene to scene. That certainly describes how I felt before I got into this study. Dreams definitely had no impact on my life because I never took the time to evaluate them. Yet our dreams, regardless of how disjointed they may appear on the surface, are important.

There is little distinction between the purpose of dreams and visions, except that dreams come when you are asleep and visions when you are awake. A vision is not just another type of daydream. Daydreams can happen on a daily basis, but visions are considered more than the images that come to your mind as daydreams. True visions do not occur on a daily basis.

The Hebrew word most used in the Bible for vision is *chazah,* which means to gaze externally and see internally an inspired appearance, or to gaze with eyes wide

21

open at something remarkable. You could be in meditation, staring into space, or you could have your eyes closed in prayer and see an inspired appearance. Then your daydream has been interrupted and has become a vision. Visions and dreams are both God-given!

Background for Natural Dreams

There are natural dreams that occur nightly, and then there are spiritual dreams. I've experienced both. Most dreams are purely natural. But there are times when one of your dreams shows you a future event or you seem to see into the spirit realm, knowing it's more than *just a dream.*

Scientists, after years of study and testing, have found that dreams are vital because they deal with our current circumstances. Dreams are a way to release the day's frustration because people work through their problems in their sleep. Scientists have found that ninety-five percent of our dreams are for us, even if someone else is featured in them.[6] Dreams are called the language of our subconscious, or they're referred to as our inner-man at work in us during sleep. It seems that in our dreams we can make rational decisions without the outside interference of the day. God knows the benefits of dreaming, and that is why He put the natural dreaming process in every person. It has nothing to do with whether or not a person is a Christian. Dreaming comes to all, regardless of age or gender. Children have the same sleep and dreaming patterns as adults. In fact, even infants in the womb have these same sleep and dreaming patterns. Evidently, the dreaming process begins before birth.[7]

Background for Spiritual Dreams

We have the potential to have spiritual dreams. Somehow, God can intervene in our natural dreaming process and cause one of our dreams to become a spiritual dream, a time when we can see into or hear from His spirit realm. It's happened to me; it's not impossible. According to the Bible, God caused natural wind to become so supernatural that it parted the Red Sea, and the children of Israel walked across on dry land (Exodus 14:21). In another event, Jesus spoke to a natural, raging storm, and it whimpered down and became calm (Mark 4:39). If this is true, then surely the Lord can make Himself known by causing a natural dream to become supernatural by speaking within it (Numbers 12:6).

I have come to understand that all dreams, whether natural or spiritual, come from our spirit. Because dreams originate in our inner man, they open us up to His spirit realm. People may consider themselves agnostic or atheistic when they are awake, but when they go to sleep, they enter into another realm, God's realm. In sleep, through the dreaming process, your inner self, your innermost being, can be revealed, and you also can become aware of His spirit realm and become God-conscious. It's exciting to know that God cares enough to reveal Himself in this way to us.

Also, I now realize that when I go to sleep I am no longer in control. A loss of control can be frightening to some, but I am not afraid because I have confidence that God is in control. He wants what is best for us.

Although God put the dreaming process in us and although dreams come from our spirit, all dreams are not spiritual dreams. God created the natural as well as the spiritual. In fact, one scientist who has helped

to interpret thousands of dreams has come to the conclusion that dreaming is "a letter from yourself to
yourself."[8]

Wake Up to Your Dreams

When you know your dreams are important, you will
become more conscious of what you have seen in your
sleep. It is true that a few dreams can be distorted due to
an upset stomach, be disturbing due to anxiety, or be
deceptive due to the enemy of our soul, who tries to dis-
rupt our dreaming process with fearful images. Some of
our dreams can become nightmares if we are not willing
to face difficult circumstances when we are awake. But
that is not the norm! Let's not leave God out! Because
dreaming is God's idea, dreams (even natural dreams)
are one of the ways we can be ministered to while we
sleep.

Dreams can be vital to our lives *if we will become
aware of our dreams!* Dreams can be free counselors,
help give direction or correction, give answers to seemingly unsolvable problems, and give comfort and
refreshing in the night.

Chapter 2

What's in a Dream?

Day unto day uttereth speech,
and night unto night sheweth knowledge.

Psalm 19:2

When I read what the psalmist said about the night and dreams, I saw that he realized our dreams can be powerful tools God can use to help us. It was such a revelation to me when I read in Psalm 19:2 about the reality of what happens in the day and in the night. We speak many words and promises during the day, and perhaps do little listening, but according to this verse, it is during the night that knowledge is shown. "Shown" (to quicken, reveal, restore, recover) is an interesting word for the psalmist to use here. It seems logical to me that this knowledge can be shown in the night through our dreams while we sleep.

Scientists tell us that we only use a small percentage of our brain capacity while awake. Perhaps we use a greater percentage of our brain capacity while we sleep. I believe that paying close attention to our dreams can show us knowledge that we may not have been aware of when we were awake.

Where Do Our Dreams Originate?

The foundation of dreams can be found at creation. When God created man in His image, He formed man from the dust then breathed into him the breath of life, and man became a "living soul" (Genesis 1:26–27; 2:7). This "living soul" part of us (the spirit of man or the God-breathed part of man) never sleeps and has God consciousness, not only when we are awake but also when we sleep. Your spirit never sleeps. Because we are created in God's image, we are three-dimensional. One minister used to have us say, "I am a spirit, I live in a body, and I have a soul."

In order to minister to our total person (spirit, soul, and body), God established the day and the night with purpose. Although we live and operate on a daily basis in this natural, physical realm, there is another realm of which to be aware. Because we are spirit beings, we are connected to the spirit realm through our spirit. We may be so busy with our activities while awake that we don't notice, but I believe that we are more open to the spirit realm as we sleep and that the awareness of another dimension can be shown to us through our dreams. It is a logical way for God, as our creator, to minister to us *Spirit-to-spirit* as we sleep. The dreams I remember have become more important to me because some of them seem to contain signals to me from the spirit realm. I do consider myself to be a very practical person, but I have to ask if there is something beyond this natural realm that we can know and experience. I believe that as we honestly evaluate our dreams, spiritual awareness and confirmation of the spirit realm can be made known to us.

How Does the Dreaming Process Work?

Because we are created in God's image and because our spirit never sleeps, it is during the time of sleep that our inner-man continues to be active. I believe that the dreaming process takes place during sleep as our inner man (subconscious) evaluates the day's situations, sorts through these circumstances, and then tries to solve problems through the natural wisdom that has come from the knowledge we received while awake (Psalm 16:7). Dreams come as a result of our spirit man's quickening our brain (our computer of stored information) to bring forth the pictures or symbols needed. When evaluated, these pictorial symbols help to give us wisdom to deal with our current circumstances. Dr. Carl Jung, an eminent Swiss psychologist, called these pictures the "inner symbols of man."[9]

Through dreams we can see the blind spots of our lives (things about ourselves that we are not aware of when we're awake) and even see inside ourselves. Our spirit man is a more powerful source than we may realize.

We obviously cannot control our dreams, though some of us may wish we could. When you go to sleep, dreams simply come. Yet it's good to know that we can try and fail in sleep, learn from mistakes, and then not have to repeat them when we are awake!

No Night in Heaven

There is a lot of fear about the night, yet when God created the night, He said it was good (Genesis 1:18). I have noted, however, that in heaven there will be no need for night. Our bodies and minds will then be perfect (incorruptible) and will never wear out (1 Corinthians 15:52). There we will need no rest, sleep, or dreams. There will be no night (Revelation 21:25; 22:5). The Lord will then speak to us face to face. No secrets will remain.

In the meantime, we need the night! While we are still here on planet Earth, we need rest, and we need wisdom to operate successfully in life. Our bodies are not perfect; God does not speak to us face to face at this time, and many times we do not get the wisdom we need while we are awake due to the many distractions. So that's where the night and dreams come in!

God's Secret Place

Much is written about the night in the Book of Psalms. Perhaps David learned about the significance of the night during his long evenings tending his father's sheep. David tells us in Psalm 18:11 that God made the darkness *His secret place.* In Psalm 91:1 we are told that "he that dwelleth in the secret place of the most High shall abide under the shadow of the Almighty."

The psalmist confirms that dreams are our inner man at work in us. In a Prayer of David, he begins, "I will bless the Lord, who hath given me counsel" (Psalm 16:7). This statement establishes that David recognized that he received divine counsel from the LORD. Then he goes on to say that he also receives counsel from his own inner self during the night. He continues, "My reins [the inner man, interior self] also instruct [correct, teach] me in the night seasons." The psalmist says that during the night, counsel is being processed through his inner man, his spirit (his reins), and he then receives instruction or wisdom as he sleeps.

> Whither shall I go from thy spirit?
> or whither shall I flee from thy presence?
> Yea, the darkness hideth not from thee;
> but the night shineth as the day:

> *the darkness and the light are both alike to thee [God].*
> *For thou hast possessed my reins:*
> *thou hast covered me in my mother's womb.*

Psalm 139:7, 12–13

The psalmist gives a concept here that we never get away from the presence of God because God was a part of our original formation at conception. God possessed (Hebrew: *ganah*—erected, created, owned) our reins (spirit, interior self, innermost being) and covered us (Hebrew: *cakak*—set, entwined, erected together, protected) before we were ever born.[10] God created our spirit man and somehow majestically entwined Himself within our inner man (reins) as we were being formed in the womb, and I believe God consciousness was being formed or set within us at that time. We were even *written in His Book* before our actual substance could be seen. Even scientists are discovering that dreaming patterns begin to operate before we are born.[11] It is no wonder the psalmist said we are fearfully and wonderfully made!

Perversion of the Night

Although God created the night and said it was good, many people hate to see night come. Satan has certainly perverted the purpose of the night. I believe Satan knows the purpose of the night, and he counterfeits and perverts what God has created because Satan has never created anything. He takes advantage of the cover of the night and sets the stage for fear because most crimes take place during this time. The Bible tells us Satan is an accuser of the brethren "day and night" (Revelation

12:10). I believe these accusations can come through tormenting dreams.

Satan tries to keep people awake when they should be sleeping because he wants people worn out to keep God out. Society goes right along with his plan; many businesses and bars are open seven days a week, twenty-four hours a day. The prophet Daniel said that the plan of the antichrist system in the last days will be to wear out the saints by changing the times and laws (Daniel 7:25).

Let me clarify something for those of you who may have to work shifts and sleep at various times. Don't think that God can only speak to you in the night. It doesn't matter when you go to sleep; the Lord knows how to minister to you through your dreams whether you are sleeping during the day or night. Anytime you sleep (day or night) you dream. The verses to which I refer about the night are indicating a time when people should be sleeping. In the Bible, the night was considered a time for sleep because they did not have our modern technology.

Blessings of the Night

I say again that you do not have to fear the night. Your sleep can be sweet because you know you dwell in the secret place of the Most High. In sleep, your heart is open before Him. None of us can play hide-and-seek with God. Jeremiah 23:24 asks, "Can any hide himself in secret places that I shall not see him? saith the LORD." David said the darkness and light are both alike to God (Psalm 139:12). Daniel understood that God "reveals the deep and secret things; He knows what is in the darkness" (Daniel 2:22 AMP). God does not simply quit speaking when we do not listen to Him in our waking hours. God is always working on our behalf. It's good to know that the night is God's secret place! The psalmist David declared, "I laid me down and slept; I awaked; for the Lord sustained me" (Psalm 3:5).

Songs in the Night

I am thankful for the hymns and good Christian music today, but some who write gospel music may not realize that God can inspire them with songs in the night, songs that are heard from the heavenly realm, birthed in their spirit, and then brought forth. I don't think it automatically happens; it does take seeking the Lord. But I believe it can happen!

King David understood the importance of having inspired heavenly music. He appointed men of skill called *seers,* ones who could see and hear into the spirit realm, to bring forth the songs of the LORD. They were to bring that heavenly music to the Tabernacle of David, and for forty years Israel experienced the songs of the Lord (1 Chronicles 25). That experience was not limited to just them or to that time. There is a promise in Acts 15:16 that the tabernacle of David will be restored in the last days and permit the return of that heavenly music. During today's new emphasis on the importance of praise and worship in the church, I wonder if we are living in that time of restoration.

In Psalm 42:8, David declared, "Yet the LORD will command his lovingkindness in the day time, and in the night His song *shall be* with me" (emphasis added). The Hebrew meaning for "song" here is joyful overflow. During the day, we can have His lovingkindness, and in the night, we can have a song of joyful overflow from the Lord. I believe this joyful overflow comes as we have put His Word in us during our waking hours. What we put into our mind and spirit while awake can filter through us as we sleep and become part of our dreams.

The psalmist in Psalm 77:6 shared the importance of the night and meditation when he said he called to remembrance his song in the night, he communed with his heart (inner feelings), and his spirit (innermost being) made diligent search. His true self was revealed.

My family had an experience that revealed to me that God can give songs in the night. Several years ago, our youngest son, Jason, was healed through a song in the night. My family had driven to Tulsa, Oklahoma, to attend the graduation of our oldest son, Jeffrey, from Rhema Bible Training Center. On Saturday, Fred took a flight back to Dayton, Ohio, so he could be at our church for the Sunday service. The kids and I stayed behind at the hotel, planning to attend church in Tulsa on Sunday and then to drive back to Dayton on Monday.

Around two o'clock that morning, as we were sleeping, Jason began to moan in his sleep. His moaning awoke my daughter, Kimberly, and me. I checked on Jason, and he was running a high fever and having difficulty breathing. Kimberly and I began to pray. I became very concerned because Jason seemed to be getting worse. I didn't have any medicine with me and thought about going to the hotel lobby to see if there might be something to relieve the fever. Just as I was getting ready to go to the lobby, Jason began to sing out in his sleep. Jason is not a singer; it shocked us when he began to sing this song:

> Speak the name; speak the mighty name of Jesus,
> for His supernatural power is still the same.
> There is power; there is healing and deliverance
> to the child of God who dares to speak the name.

He sang beautifully, and his song permeated the atmosphere. The presence of the Lord filled the room. Kimberly and I began to cry and just bask in the Lord's presence. Kimberly then asked, "Mom, is Jason still asleep?" I checked on him, and he was still sleeping. With our crying and praising the Lord so loudly, I don't know how Jason managed to stay asleep, but he did. What happened next amazed us as much as Jason's singing out in his sleep. As I looked at Jason, his fever suddenly broke, his rapid breathing ceased, and he turned over and slept the rest of the night. Kim and I continued to thank the Lord for what had happened until we, too, fell asleep.

The next morning, as we were getting ready for church, Jason was being a typical boy. He was jumping from bed to bed and having a ball—no sign of sickness. I stopped him and asked him if he knew the song "Speak the Name."

He said, "No, Mom, I don't know that song."

I then asked him if he remembered being sick during the night. He replied, "No, Mom. Was I sick?"

I then shared with him that he had been sick during the night and that he sang that beautiful song. He listened intently, and I could tell he was touched. But being a cool kid, he didn't want to show too much emotion. That morning we attended a church where the guest speaker was Ed Cole, an evangelist whose ministry was primarily to men. At the close of his challenging message, he gave a call to men to make a commitment to God. He asked those who wanted to be mighty men of God to lift their hands. I felt Jason moving next to me. I looked over, and Jason was crying as he lifted his hand in response to the call. Then the evangelist told the men who really meant business with God to stand to their feet and cry out to the Lord to help them to be the men that God wanted them to be. Suddenly, Jason jumped to his feet and lifted both of his hands in the air, and with tears streaming down his face, he began to cry out to the Lord that he wanted to be a mighty man of God.

I can remember that day clearly. He was just a young boy, standing in the second row of that large church with his hands raised toward heaven and crying out that he wanted to be a mighty man of God. He seemed so insignificant, and I'm sure Ed Cole did not notice that small boy in the second row. But the Lord did. Not only had the message touched our son's heart that morning; the Lord also had prepared him during the night. Truly, the Lord had given Jason His song in the night. As I have continued to study about the purpose of the night, I have come to realize what happened to our son. Jason had heard that song as we played the tape in our car while driving to Tulsa. The musical message had gone into his spirit. We had played many tapes during the fourteen-hour drive, and Jason had not remembered that particular song. (To tell you the truth, I had not remembered it either.) But when healing was needed, the Lord brought forth the message of that song out of Jason's spirit, and, as he slept, he was healed. The Lord knew the song of faith that was needed. Because of that experience during the night, the next morning Jason was open to receive the word from the man of God. God does give songs in the night, and you can never convince my daughter or me that He doesn't.

Ephesians 5:19 states that we are to speak to ourselves when we are awake in psalms (Scriptures sung), hymns (praise and worship), and spiritual (Holy Spirit-breathed) songs, singing and making melody in our hearts to the Lord. What are you listening to during the day? You can never go wrong by filling yourself with the Word, no matter if it is written, spoken, or sung. What Jason had put into his mind and spirit brought forth healing in the time of need.

I encourage you to ask the Lord to give you His songs in the night! Pray over your own sleep and pray over the sleep of your loved ones. May we say along with the psalmist, "Yet the LORD will command His lovingkindness [deeds of mercy] in the daytime, and in the night his song [joyful overflow] shall be with me, and my prayer [hymn of intercession] unto the God of my life" (Psalm 42:8). You too can have sweet sleep and dreams of refreshing.

Chapter 3

God's Gift of Dreams to You

It is vain for you to rise up early,
to take rest late,
to eat the bread of (anxious) toil—
for He gives (blessings) to His beloved in sleep.

Psalm 127:2 (AMP)

When I first began teaching on dreams, one of the men in our church shared with me that he worked with scientists, most of whom were either atheistic or agnostic, who had learned to rely on their dreams. He went on to say that these scientists kept pads of paper and pens next to their beds. When one of the scientists was struggling to find an answer to a certain project, he or she would go home early and "sleep on it." Amazingly, many times these scientists would get their answers as they slept. After he heard my teaching, the man in our church then understood why these scientists depended on their dreams. If these scientists can make discoveries through their dreams, we, too, can receive answers through our dreams! These scientists meditated on the need and then depended on their natural dreams to give solutions to natural situations. Perhaps all of us need to learn to "sleep on it" when we're going through a rough time and need answers.

The Purpose of Natural Dreams

Not only are spiritual dreams a gift from God, so are natural dreams. Given the amount of time we all spend dreaming, dreams may be our most underutilized resources. Scientists say dreaming helps us to be sane and healthy. No matter what we dream about, a normal night's dream cycle refreshes the brain, sorts out information, improves our eye coordination, and helps to maintain physical health. We don't even have to recall a dream to get that wonderful benefit. It's automatic.[12]

Now that I better understand the purpose of my dreams, I know I can receive solutions to everyday situations as my "inner man," my subconscious, sorts through the information of the day and brings forth wisdom through my dreams while I sleep. Going to sleep has become a great stress reliever for me. When I awake, before I even get out of bed, I begin to thank the Lord for the wisdom He gave me while I was sleeping—even if I do not recall my dreams.

To emphasize this wonderful gift further, I have found that great discoveries have been made through dreams! I read the story of a man who had been working on his new invention for years and had become very discouraged. He had tried everything he knew to do, and nothing seemed to work. One night after feverishly working all day, he fell asleep and had a dream during the night. In his dream, he was in a jungle and was captured by savages who put him in a pot of boiling water. They danced around him, threatening to kill him if he did not finish his invention. Terrified, he looked out from the pot of boiling water and noticed these savages were holding long, pointed spears. Holes were near the tips of their spears, and he saw a thin cloth running through these holes to connect the spears. As they danced, they were lifting their spears up and down.

He awoke, thinking he had had a crazy dream or nightmare. He went back to work on his invention, but he kept thinking about the dream. As he worked on his invention and meditated on his dream, he realized his dream had revealed how to complete his new invention! The man's name was Elias Howe; his dream helped him figure out where to put the eye of the needle on his new invention—*the sewing machine.*[13]

Many of us would have laughed about a crazy dream like that of Elias Howe or would have awakened in fear due to such a terrible nightmare. But Howe made a great discovery by listening to his dream.

There are others who have made discoveries as they slept. Niels Bohr, upon accepting his Nobel Prize, declared that his dreams had shown him the structure of the atom. It is said that the theory of relativity came to Einstein in either a dream or vision. Apparently, he saw it on a beam of light. The design for the first radio tube also came to the inventor in a dream. You golfers will love this—Jack Nicklaus dreamed of a new golf grip that made a winning difference in his game.[14]

These men had been studying and experimenting to find solutions while they were awake and could not finish their inventions until the answers came in their sleep. I wonder how many of us may have let great inventions or solutions to serious problems slip by us because we did not evaluate the message of our dreams.

The Purpose of Spiritual Dreams

Certainly, spiritual dreams are a gift from the Lord. A dream is spiritual if it reveals something to you that you have no way of knowing by yourself. God wants to help us when we cannot help ourselves. I want to emphasize that you cannot *make* a spiritual dream happen. It happens at the will of God.

Through my studies and in evaluating spiritual dreams, I see the pattern of the inner workings of the

Spirit within me as I sleep. While I am asleep, my sub-conscious reviews the day's situations. Sometimes, however, when it is searching for answers, none appear. I cannot come up with an answer because I do not have that knowledge within me. I need divine wisdom or a divine answer that only God can give, and God in His mercy intervenes in my dreaming process to give that wisdom in the form of a spiritual dream.

This same process can be true with you also. When you need a divine answer, the Holy Spirit, through divine energy, deposits within you (your inner man) the needed wisdom or revelation. Your spirit then quickens your brain to bring forth the symbols or pictures to reveal information or answers that you did not have. Therefore, there is a divine revelation. This divine revelation can be the showing of a future event, the imparting of information that you would have no way of knowing, the showing of symbols that give you warning, the revealing of the spirit realm, or the refreshing and encouraging that you needed. This information comes supernaturally.

David understood that God made divine deposits within him while he slept. He said that "the Lord proved his heart and visited him and tried him in the night" (Psalm 17:3). When I studied in my concordance the Hebrew meaning of this verse, I got excited. I found that this Scripture reveals that our Creator cares enough about us to "prove" (investigate) our "heart" (motives), "visit" us (oversee and make a divine deposit within) and then "try" us (purge and refine as a goldsmith) in those areas within us needing to be cleansed. And this is done even as we sleep! How can the Lord do all these things? I believe He does this through the dreaming process.

It sure seems as if there is a lot going on inside of us while we sleep, doesn't it? We're watched over, tested, purged, and refined. I hope this doesn't overwhelm you, but I want you to realize that what happens within you while you sleep is not bad; it is a blessing.

After reading this, can you begin to see that you do not have to solve your problems alone? There are occasions when we may not be able to face our situations or ourselves, and there are times when God does not get our attention while we are awake. But God sees the real us and our real needs, so sleep becomes a time when He can visit us and impart within us what is needed as He intervenes into our natural dreaming process! This information almost makes you want to go "sleep on it," doesn't it?

Background to Symbols in Dreams

We dream in pictures, not in words, and we remember more of what we see than what we hear. I encourage you to evaluate these symbolic pictures to see whether or not they are natural or spiritual in nature. However, I do caution you that it is not wise to *spiritualize* everything you dream or every thought that comes to your mind. In reality, pictures are passing through our brain all the time. We can see pictures any time we close our eyes.

Circumstances can affect our dreams and our imagination. I've conducted an experiment in some of the seminars at which I have spoken. I have had the students close their eyes, and while their eyes are closed, I describe images such as chocolate ice cream double-dipped on a sugar cone, red convertibles, kisses, children, or flowers. Afterward, I ask them if the pictures changed in their mind as I mentioned these different words. And the pictures do change. The pictures change as their thoughts change according to the images I describe.

The same is true in the dreaming process. What you have seen or experienced during the day will affect the symbols of your dreams as your inner man processes these images during sleep. When you recall what you have seen in your sleep, these symbols can catch your attention and make you think. The stories of your dreams are usually principle-oriented and deal with your situation and with the real you. After remembering your dream, you will either evaluate or ignore what you've seen in your sleep.

I've discovered that the stories of our dreams are similar to the parables of Jesus. Jesus shared parables that spoke to the hearts of people while they were awake, and dreams speak to the hearts of people while they are sleeping. In Matthew 13:10–17, Jesus said that the people did not understand His parables because the people were inwardly dull of hearing. People do not understand their dreams for the same reason.

People who do not know to take dreams seriously feel it is a waste of time to even think about their dreams. They become dull of hearing inwardly. When a dream reveals something important, they don't even realize it. The more they ignore the symbolic parables of their dreams, the easier ignoring becomes. Then dreams lose their purpose. The Bible says that God's people can be destroyed due to a lack of knowledge (Hosea 4:6).

Think about the symbols of your dream as they skip from image to image; you need to discern what you have seen in your sleep. What mystery is it revealing? What are you going through at the present time that the dream may be dealing with? What are your feelings?

We as Christians should go to sleep expecting and be more open to recognizing spiritual dreams. The Lord wants to give His people "the treasures of darkness"

(Isaiah 45:3). Psalm 127:2 says, "He giveth his beloved sleep," and another version says, "He gives (blessings) to His beloved in sleep" (AMP). Song of Solomon 5:2 states, "I sleep, but my heart (inner man) waketh: it is the voice of my beloved." You do not have to solve your problems alone. Jesus said in Matthew 28:20, "Lo, I am with you always," and that means even during your sleep.

Circumstances Affect Dreams

It is true that dreams can be affected by what is happening to us as we sleep. We may eat something that upsets our stomach and causes us to have a distorted dream. Circumstances during our sleep may even cause us to think our dream is spiritual when it is not. For the most part though, dreams can give us in-depth revelation regardless of the circumstances surrounding our sleep.

A friend of mine shared a dream with me—a dream that he thought at first was surely a spiritual dream. In the dream, he was being crucified with Jesus. Surely, he thought, that had to be a spiritual dream; he even realized in the dream that he was dreaming. He said as he was laid out on a cross and as his hands were being nailed to it, he could feel the excruciating pain of the nails going into his hands. In the dream, he thought, "This is so spiritual. I am being crucified with Jesus." Then, as the nails were being driven deeper into his hands, he awoke. What a spiritual dream, he thought. He had dreamed of being crucified with Jesus, and he could still feel the pain in his hand. Then his mind cleared. "Why am I still feeling this pain if that was just a dream?" Then he realized what had happened.

That night, before going to bed, his wife had rolled her hair and had put plastic picks in the rollers to keep them in place. During the night, she had rolled over on his hand, and one of those picks had stuck into his hand. He had dreamed he was being crucified as a result of his pain. When he awoke and looked at his hand, he saw his wife's head lying on it and her pick sticking into his hand. He was so upset that the dream wasn't as spiritual as he had thought. He woke up his wife to inform her of what she had done. Needless to say, she never used those plastic picks again.

I don't know if I would consider that dream spiritual, but it did show what was in this man's heart. He dreamed he was being crucified with Christ as a result of the pain in his hand. It might not have been a spiritual dream, but it did reveal that he was spiritually minded.

Déjà Vu

Been there, done that. But when and where?

Most of us would admit that we've been in a situation in which we realized that things were familiar, but we knew that we had never physically been in that place before. I've come to the conclusion that *déjà vu* comes because we dreamed about something *before it happened.* You may not remember or write down a dream, but circumstances can bring back to you portions of the dream.

Historians tell us that two weeks before his death in 1865, Abraham Lincoln dreamed that he entered the East Room of the White House and found a body laid out in state. A guard told him that the president had been assassinated.[15]

43

Personal Dreams of the Future

I've had several dreams that showed me future events about which I would have had no other way of knowing beforehand. Dreams have revealed to me certain situations that people in our church were going through. Usually I do not approach the people but know that I am to pray. There's one particular dream, however, in which I did sense the need to talk with the people.

Several years ago on a Saturday night, I had a dream about one of the couples in our church. In the dream, they were sitting in their home, talking about leaving our church to go to another church across town. It was as if I were peering into their living room and overhearing them as they shared with each other where they were going and why. Then the scene changed, and I was alone with the wife in a field. I was talking with her about their move and sharing my concern. She kept assuring me that everything was okay, but as she was talking to me, she also was walking away from me. Suddenly, she started going down an embankment. As I reached out to her, it was if I was in slow motion, and our fingers almost touched. Yet she continued to slip down the embankment.

I awoke concerned in the middle of the night, and I knew this family was going to leave our church. I felt sick inside. They were good people, and I did not want them to leave; however, I was even more concerned about the latter part of the dream. In the morning, I told Fred that this family was leaving our church. When he asked me how I knew this, I told him I had dreamed it. He laughed a cautious laugh and said, "Well, we'll see. I hope it's not true." I could tell by his eyes that he already knew it was true.

That Sunday morning that family was not in church. I talked to a friend of the family, and she thought they were on vacation. Relieved, I put the dream on the shelf. The next Sunday that couple was once again not in church. I really did not want to call them, and I certainly did not want to share the dream. As I said, unless I sense a tremendous urging, I do not share my dreams with others.

Well, that dream would not leave my mind, and I felt such urgency that I called them that Sunday afternoon. Hesitantly, I made small talk with the wife for a minute and let her know that I had missed her in church. Then I told her why I was calling—that I could not get away from a dream I had had. I briefly shared the dream with her and said, "If this dream doesn't mean anything to you, just forget it." There was silence on the other end. I waited.

Finally, she responded, "I don't know what to say. It's as if you were sitting in our living room last Saturday and overheard our conversation. We have told no one that we're leaving the church or what other church we'll attend. In fact, we visited that church today. We feel we need to be in a smaller church, and we were going to talk with you about it later. I just don't know what to say, except that we feel that this is God's will for our family."

I assured her that I was not calling to talk her family into staying in our church. It was their decision. I cautioned her, though, and asked her to pray about the dream. She said that everything was fine with them and that I shouldn't worry. We then hung up, and it was over; they were gone. Every time I thought of them that dream nagged me, but eventually, I forgot about it.

As time went on, I learned that this couple left the other church, too, and went through a divorce. The family has experienced much pain. Not long ago, a friend of the family told me that the wife had asked her to give me a message. Her message to me was this: "I wish to God I had heeded that dream. It was truly a dream from

God." Then, a few months ago, I saw her myself, coming down the aisle of our church. Tears were in our eyes as we hugged. She spoke quietly in my ear, "Everything you saw in that dream has come to pass. I'll never forget you. Remember my family and me when you pray." She left immediately after church, and we didn't get to talk further. However, she and her family are still in my thoughts and prayers.

It wasn't a coincidence that I had that dream the very night that they had their conversation. I could have never thought that up myself. We pastor a large church, and I certainly was not thinking about this family. No one had talked with me about them. As far as I knew, everything was fine. But God knew this family needed help, and He intervened into my natural dreaming process to reveal information I had no other way of knowing in order to warn this family what would happen to them if they continued on their course. That's the depth of the love of God. I foresaw in the dream an event unknown to me, and the dream came to pass. The purpose of this dream was not only to caution but to draw this family back to God through the revelation of a supernatural dream.

I had another interesting experience when Fred and I attended a small, intimate retreat for pastors and their wives. One evening the host asked me to share about dreams. At the close of my teaching, we all prayed over our sleep, and I told them that I expected them to remember and share one of their dreams the next morning. At the morning session, one of the pastors told us that he had dreamed that the cook for the retreat had a heart attack and was taken to the hospital by ambulance, although the cook did not die. We immediately prayed about his dream and for John, our cook.

During lunch that very day, we heard a noise in the kitchen as pans hit the floor. We ran to the kitchen, and John was lying on the floor, gasping for breath as he held his chest. Someone immediately dialed 911. A few of us who could fit in the kitchen gathered around him. I overhead the pastor who had had the dream say to John, "You'll be all right. I dreamed about you last night, and we prayed. Don't be afraid." An ambulance took John to the hospital, where he was examined by the doctors, and was with us again in a couple of days.

That event impacted all of us. I don't know how sensitive this pastor would have been to his dream if he had not heard a teaching on dreams the day before. Would John have survived the heart attack if the pastor had not remembered his dream and if we had not prayed? I'm sure he would have. But I also believe that the prayer before the incident and the encouragement John received in the midst of it increased his faith and his ability to recover quickly.

A dream can impact you so much that it causes a turning point in your life. John Newton, captain of a slave trade vessel in the 1800s, had a terrifying dream that overwhelmed him. A few years later, he was dramatically converted to Christ, and it was then that he realized the powerful dream had foretold his conversion. He became a pastor, helped to abolish the slave trade, and is best known as the author of "Amazing Grace." He taught that people who believe the Bible know that some dreams are communications from heaven, guiding us or foretelling the future, and that such dreams come to God's people.[16]

Prepare to Hear from God

If you want to receive wisdom from your inner man or know when you have heard from God in your sleep, you must not allow your thinking to be influenced by the tradition of our Western culture or even by church tradition that implies dreams are of no value. Pray over your sleep. Awake slowly, recalling your thoughts. Recognize that your dreams are important and desire to learn from them. Don't ignore them. Write them down! Evaluate them! Heed them!

Let me caution you that, even though I value dreams, I do not believe that dreams are the only way you can receive wisdom or that they are the only way God can reveal Himself to you. Do not get so excited about dreams that you begin to seek for God to speak to you through dreams. Don't seek dreams. Seek God!

God can speak to us in various ways. Certainly, the written Word, the Bible, is the most profound way that God speaks to us. Second Timothy 3:16 says, "All scripture is given by inspiration of God, and is profitable for doctrine, for reproof, for correction, for instruction in righteousness." The Bible also says that we can be led by God's Spirit and that if we are we will not fulfill the lust of the flesh (Galatians 5:16–18). The Lord can speak to us through His ministers. Jesus has given to the church some apostles, prophets, evangelists, pastors, and teachers for the perfecting (maturing) of the saints (Ephesians 4:11).

God can manifest His power and wisdom through the gifts of the Holy Spirit. These gifts are listed in 1 Corinthians 12:8–10: word of wisdom, word of knowledge, discerning of spirits, working of miracles, gifts of healing, faith, divers tongues, interpretation of tongues, and prophecy. Of course, the Lord also can deal with us and reveal Himself through natural circumstances. He has given us common sense, a mind, to figure things out. In Psalm 37:23, we are told that the steps of a good man are ordered by the Lord. The Bible tells us to study to show ourselves approved. He has given us natural wisdom to go along with natural circumstances!

Please realize that dreams are only one of the tools the Lord can use, and He has other ways to aid us. He will guide us when we are awake as we are sensitive to Him and even when we are asleep as we receive direction through God's gift of dreams.

4

The Bible Speaks
of Natural Dreams

For a dream cometh through the multitude of business . . .

Ecclesiastes 5:3

Before I started studying dreams, I didn't realize that the Bible has something to say about natural dreams. But I've found that the Bible is not only a spiritual book but also a practical and scientific book. Solomon, one of the wisest men who ever lived, shared some of his wisdom about dreams. He said in Ecclesiastes 5:3, "For a dream cometh through the multitude of business." He let us know that dreams come as a result of the business of the day—our daily activities. In other words, Solomon said, dreams deal with our current circumstances, confirming what scientists have recently proved.

Solomon continued, "In the multitude of dreams and many words there are also divers vanities: but fear thou God" (Ecclesiastes 5:7). Dreams, even as much talking, are not taken seriously. When people ramble on and on, they aren't weighing their words carefully. Then those who have to listen to these talkers do not take their words seriously. The same is true with dreams. Dreams come every night, and they can become vain because people simply quit paying attention to them. Because their dreams seem to ramble, people ignore them. If you do not weigh your dream carefully, your dream loses its value and purpose because it is not interpreted.

Solomon's main emphasis here is to fear God. As you reverence God, He will cause you to become more aware of your conversation during the day and of your dreams during the night. Your conversation will become more effective, and as the Lord binds those dreams firmly upon your heart, you will remember them.

Dreams that Deal with Current Situations

Isaiah prophesied that Israel's distress would be as "a dream of a night vision. It shall even be as when an hungry man dreameth, and, behold, he eateth; but he awaketh, and his soul is empty: or as when a thirsty man dreameth, and, behold, he drinketh; but he awaketh, and, behold, he is faint, and his soul hath appetite" (Isaiah 29:7–8). Isaiah compares Israel's problems to those of a hungry man who dreams of eating food, but when he awakes, he is still hungry unless he eats! In other words, his natural body is not satisfied through a dream. When the man awakes, he still must take action and eat or drink. The same was true with the people of Israel; they were given instructions for what to do, but they did not do it.

This Scripture parallels Israel with those who ignore the message of their dreams. When we have a dream that gives us direction, it is up to us as individuals to take whatever action is necessary. Dreams alone will not solve our problems. It is the action we take when we awake that brings a solution to our situation.

What you do during the day affects your dreams. Jude, the half brother of Jesus, let us know that dreams can become filthy due to vain thoughts and actions during the day. In verse 8, Jude said, "Likewise also these filthy dreamers defile the flesh, despise dominion [government], and speak evil of dignities [those due respect]."

Their dreams became filthy due to what they did during their waking hours: defile, despise, and speak evil.

Today pornography is easily available, and violence fills movies and television. A person's innocence is quickly stolen. If we dwell on negative and perverse thoughts, our spirit man becomes weakened and darkened by what it has been fed during the day. Even scientists have proved that dreams can change according to a person's environment or surroundings (Winter 1989).

In writing to the church at Rome, which was surrounded by heathens, the apostle Paul declared, "Because that, when they knew God, they glorified him not as God, neither were thankful; but became vain in their imaginations, and their foolish heart was darkened" (Romans 1:21). Paul let the church know that because the people of that day refused to acknowledge God, their imaginations (thoughts) became vain and their hearts (inner man) darkened and dull. It was a process. When this happened, it also affected their night season, sleep, and dreams. Dreams became darkened because they now came from the deceit of the heart (Jeremiah 23).

Do not think that because you are surrounded by a negative environment during the day, you will have a fearful time during the night as you sleep. Jude verse 20 says, "But ye, beloved, building up yourselves on your most holy faith, praying in the Holy Ghost." You can build yourself up during the day regardless of your surroundings, and it definitely will affect what occurs during your sleep.

Dreams that Are Not Remembered

Scientists tell us we have an average of four dreams per night.[17] However, most people are not aware of their dreams unless they are terrifying ones that wake them up. Even then, dreams may not be taken seriously. Many people wake up to loud alarm clocks, rush to the bathroom to get a shower, get dressed, and then grab a piece of toast on their way out the door to work. Is it any wonder they never think about what they may have dreamed during the night?

Both Job and the psalmist agree that most dreams are not remembered. These writers compared ignoring a dream to the fleeting thoughts people have when the wicked perish (see Job 20:5–8). The psalmist says, "As a dream when one awaketh; so, O Lord, when thou awakest, thou shalt despise their image" (Psalm 73:20). Our dreams can become despised or easily forgotten even as the wicked are despised and forgotten. When people let their dreams fade from memory, the situation is similar to the way people react when the wicked die. No one asks. No one seems to care.

God wants us to remember our dreams. He would not have put the dreaming process within us if dreams had no purpose. Who knows what wisdom, direction, or inventions may have been lost due to forgotten dreams? I know I have let a lot of my dreams slip away from me, but I don't want to despise any more of my dreams and cause them to lose their purpose! I'm asking the Lord to help me make up for lost time, for He is the God of restoration; I believe if you will ask Him, He will help you to make up for any of your lost dreams.

Nightmares

I've talked to people who have had the same dream for years. They may not dream the exact dream every night—some of the symbols may change—but periodically the same principle of the dream keeps coming back to them. Repeated dreams can become nightmares. If you are having recurring dreams, they usually indicate that there is something you fear, that there is a situation you are not facing when you are awake, or that there are circumstances you may not know how to face when you are awake.

The Bible gives us some understanding about nightmares in the Book of Job. In the midst of Job's time of testing, he brought an accusation against God and said, "Thou scarest me with dreams, and terrifiest me through visions: so that my soul chooseth strangling, and death rather than life" (Job 7:14–15). Job was in bad shape. He wanted to die rather than have another fearful dream. He was going through a terrible time of loss and sickness. But were these nightmares from God? Job certainly thought so, for he said, "Thou, [God], scarest me." Personally, I do not believe these nightmares were from God. These nightmares were indications of Job's struggle when he was awake.

Scientists tell us that dreams can become nightmares when a person is unable to cope with situations while awake. This was truly the case with Job. He was in a life-and-death struggle when he was awake, and he did not know why. He was also surrounded by judgmental friends who gave him no hope. Therefore, in the night he had dreams that became terrifying nightmares, coming from his tormented spirit man. His dreams became fearful due to his present situation; therefore, he blamed God.

Whenever we are in a stressful situation, it affects our sleep. We have either insomnia due to worry or troubling dreams as our inner man tries to work through a solution to our dilemma. How can we have that sweet sleep that is promised us? It comes as we have confidence in our God, confidence that He wants what is best for us and that as we pray He will give us wisdom to walk through whatever our situation may be. He can bring about a change in our circumstances like the turning of a page or a new chapter in a book. It's interesting to me that Job later repented to God because he recognized his wrong thinking, and he even prayed for his misguided, comforting friends. Everything Job lost was restored double by God. I believe that his sleep also was restored and became sweet. The page was turned, and Job started a new chapter in life.

The psalmist David wrote, "I will both lay me down in peace, and sleep: for thou, LORD, only makest me dwell in safety" during a time when he was running from King Saul, who wanted to kill him (Psalm 4:8). David's confidence was in the Lord, so he could lie down and sleep during that stressful time. David did not lose sleep over Saul. God not only spared David but elevated him to the position of king.

False Dreams

Not all dreams reveal truth. In fact, I recently dreamed that my daughter, Kimberly, who was expecting a baby any day, had a baby girl. The next day I received a call from my son-in-law, Greg, informing me that a baby boy was born. I wasn't disappointed, just surprised. I already have a grandson; I think maybe in my heart I wanted a granddaughter, and that's why I had dreamed she had a girl. This was a simple dream, but I think it proves a point. I've heard people say that whenever you remember a dream, don't take it seriously because the opposite takes place. That is not always true either.

The Bible does let us know that there can be false dreams that come from the deceitful desires of people's hearts. Secret desires, false information, or perversion that people put into their mind and spirit while they are awake can affect their dreams. The prophet Zechariah warned the people of his day that false prophets saw lies and told false dreams of comfort to a sinful people because there were no strong shepherds—men who had a pastor's heart for the people. These false prophets were the psychics of that day. These shepherds did not teach the people the truth or warn them against the false. No doubt these shepherds were bound by fear of the people. They tried to please the people, and the results were devastating to the people and to the nation of Israel. These false dreams drew the people *away* from God, not *to* God. Even today you can judge the truth of a dream by evaluating whether or not it edifies you with right principles and draws you toward the Lord (Jeremiah 23:24–32; Zechariah 10:2).

Through the years, I have had several people share with me that they felt they had a dream that confirmed it was all right for them to have an affair or to take some other action that is not morally right. When I would question them further, I have usually found that their dream had come as a result of what they had been meditating on or actions they were already taking. It doesn't take me long to help those people interpret their dreams. I feel these dreams do not come from God but from people's own selfish desires. Knowing the principles of the Word of God can help people understand the true nature of their dreams.

In Deuteronomy, Moses said that if a dream is accompanied by a sign but the message draws people away from God, the dream should be ignored. In those days, a prophet could be put to death for telling a false dream that caused a nation to sin (Deuteronomy 13:1–5).

God judged Israel when the people believed a false dream. If they believed a false dream and sinned, it proved they did not love the Lord with all their heart and soul. He doesn't want people saying that He spoke to them through a dream if He did not. In fact, the Bible says God is against the person who tells false dreams (Jeremiah 23:32). It's evident that God takes dreams very seriously.

I'm not trying to put fear in you about dreams, but I want to help you realize how seriously dreams were considered in biblical times. Even today, if people say they have had a dream for you, carefully observe the principle of the dream. When a dream is for you, it should confirm something in your spirit; there should be a *yes* feeling on the inside. If it's not for you, their dream may be for them alone.

I've had people tell me that I was in their dream and that its message was for me. I usually have the person write out the dream, so they and I can evaluate it. If I do not believe their dream is for me, I tell them. I don't want to hurt their feelings, but I want to show them that they need to be more cautious about sharing their dreams as if the dreams were for others. There have been times when I felt others' dreams were for me, and I have thanked them for sharing with me. Often, however, the dream reveals their true, maybe hidden feelings toward me. That can be an eye-opener!

People must understand that even if another person is featured in their dream, it still may not be for that other person. The Bible gives only a few references of people's dreams being for someone else. If people are not sensitive to their own dreams, God may speak to someone else through a dream about them. This situation took place with the prophet Nathan and King David (2 Samuel 12).

Dreams have helped solve problems. Practical knowledge came when Joseph interpreted Pharaoh's dream, and Joseph had Egypt store up grain for seven years before famine came (Genesis 41). Peter received insight into his own prejudice when his true feelings toward the Gentiles were revealed through a dream (Acts 10:34). On the other hand, false dreams from ungodly prophets created problems for the nation of Israel, according to Jeremiah and Zechariah. Dreams were important then even as they are today.

Summarizing the Bible's Wisdom about Natural Dreams

Let's pull these Scriptures together to get some insight into natural dreaming. Moses, Jeremiah, and Zechariah gave warnings that dreams should be carefully evaluated to see whether they are drawing us toward right principles or away from them. Both Solomon and Jude said that dreams come as a result of the business of our day, which lets us know that our meditation and daily activities do affect our sleep and dreams. Isaiah shared that our dreams will not be of benefit to us if we do not heed them when we awake. Job was an example to us of why nightmares come. The psalmist encouraged us not to despise our dreams by letting them slip from us. It's good to know that the Bible is also a practical book about the subject of dreams.

Chapter 5

Science Speaks
of Natural Dreams

My reins also instruct me in the night seasons.

Psalm 16:7

In the 1950s, American scientists had a breakthrough in their study of dreams. They began to set up sleep labs to monitor the dreams of both adults and children. It was through these studies that scientists discovered that our sleep periods are extremely regular.[18]

Measuring Dreams

In sleep labs, scientists have measured the dreams of the sleeping person by attaching electrodes to the brain and monitoring the brain waves. They discovered that the brain of a sleeping person is active during dreaming. After monitoring a dream and awakening the sleeping person, scientists noted that a dreamer can vividly recall his or her dream. The easier way to measure a dream is to observe people's eyes, which move as they *watch* their dream. When their eyes quit moving, their dream is over.

People do dream *every* night whether or not they recall their dreams. It's been proven that people have four to six dreams each night, and each dream averages fifteen to twenty minutes. Through scientific study, dream experts have discovered that there are three stages in sleep: shallow, dreaming, and then deep sleep. We move through these stages every ninety minutes or so. Because this process repeats itself during sleep, you may feel that you have tossed and turned all night. In shallow sleep, you are either going into sleep or coming out of sleep. In the dreaming process, your inner man is at work in you. Then comes deep sleep and rest.[19]

REM

The movement of a sleeping person's eyes during sleep is called rapid eye movement (REM). REM usually lasts an average of fifteen to twenty minutes per cycle, and we have about four to six REM periods a night. During REM periods, people experience body changes such as rapid breathing, increased heart rate and blood pressure, sweating, and brain activity, yet they are unable to move their body.

When people are coming out of REM and are semi-awake, they are aware of what is happening around them but cannot move. Things may seem distorted. Sometimes this is because they are still in the dream stage and are between the two worlds of being asleep and being awake. During this time, their body is adjusting to waking up.[20]

As I'm awaking from a dream, sometimes I hear strange noises and think someone is in my room. I try to talk or wake up or get up, and I can't do anything. I feel paralyzed and can't move; it's a terrible feeling. Since I have done this study, however, I have become more aware of this stage of sleep. Now when I start waking up and sense something happening around me, I don't panic. I've had numerous people question me about this experience because they did not understand it. One person thought it was some type of demonic attack. I assure you that it is not. After I shared this stage of sleep, the demons seemingly disappeared

The question has been asked me several times, "Do blind people see in their dreams?" Those born blind do dream and experience auditory imagery (sounds, temperature sensations, touch), but not visual imagery. The majority of those who go blind before age five will not have visual dreams. People who lose their sight between ages five and seven continue to experience some visual imagery, but the content is about former situations rather than new ones.[21]

The Psychological Dream Theory

There are two opposing scientific theories in dream research today. One theory is that dreams come from the psychological, subconscious, or unconscious mind, and the other is that dreams are strictly biological. Sigmund Freud, who published his classic book *The Interpretation of Dreams* in 1900, felt that dreams show our inward motives because they reflect the feelings and thoughts of our subconscious mind. Freud made a simple yet penetrating observation: Dreamers who are encouraged to talk about their dream symbols and the thoughts these symbols prompt will eventually reveal the subconscious background of their struggles.

Carl G. Jung, an eminent Swiss psychologist who practiced in Switzerland from 1909 to 1961, was one of the founders of analytic psychology. He introduced the familiar terms extrovert and introvert. He completed his final book, *Man and His Symbols,* just ten days before his death. The book is a collective effort with a group of his closest followers that attempts to explain his concepts on dreams. Jung, who spent more than fifty years investigating dream symbols, came to the conclusion that dreams and their symbols are not stupid and meaningless. On the contrary, dreams provide interesting information for those who take the time to understand them.

Jung wrote, "In a period of human history when all available energy is spent in the investigation of nature, very little attention is paid to the essence of man—his unconscious or inner man. It is through this essence that symbols are produced, and it is also through this essence that God is able to speak through dreams."[22]

Dr. Calvin Hall, former director of the Institute of Dream Research in Santa Cruz, California and author of *The Meaning of Dreams,* has collected more than thirty thousand dreams. His conclusion is that "dreams are a personal letter to one's self."[23] By realizing our dreams and studying them, we look inside ourselves.

The Biological Dream Theory

Others say that dreams are biological or strictly physical. Dr. Robert McCarley, co-director of the Laboratory of Neurophysiology at Massachusetts Mental Health and associate professor of Harvard University, believes that the brain creates its own electrical energy during dreaming. This electrical energy stimulates the various parts of the brain, and the visual product (dreams) is part of the brain activity, explaining why the pictures change radically.[24] I believe this energy comes from the spirit of man.

Most scientists do not believe dreams are just a random collection of thoughts and nerve impulses; most think that dreams are a vital part of man. What you dream is not entirely divorced from who you are. Scientists also have found that even nightmares are important. These dreams may, in fact, be revealing a hidden part of ourselves, a part we do not want to face when awake. As we begin to understand what those nightmares represent to us and face them, our waking lives will be enriched.[25]

Lucid Dreaming

Lucid means that dreamers are aware that they are dreaming and can control some of their actions during the dream; this was a discovery first made by the Dutch psychiatrist Frederik van Eeden in 1913. Stephen LaBerge of the Research Association at Stanford University Psychiatry Department has done research on lucid dreaming. Dr. LaBerge believes that with practice a person can induce lucid dreaming and can stop recurring nightmares.

I have experienced a few lucid dreams, and I know a lady who goes back to sleep and changes her dream if she doesn't have a good feeling about it. However, I've never been able to do that, and I have never met anyone else who is able to do it.

In his study, Dr. LaBerge brought in volunteer dreamers called *oneironauts* or *oneiros,* the Greek words for dream. He wanted to have these people signal with their eyes as he talked to them during their dreams, and he used a polysomnograph to measure their dreams. He felt that if people could become aware that they were dreaming, they could change some actions in their dreams.

For example, a person who is running in fear from an animal in the dream could realize that he or she was dreaming and then stop and face that animal. The result should be that the fear this person was struggling with while awake would disappear.

Although the results sound good, LaBerge has received little support for his study because dream experts have found that ninety-eight percent of dreams are not lucid.[26] I do not believe God wants us to be in control during our dreams. As it is, many of us try to take control of too much while we are awake.

Dream Testing

Scientists have conducted many tests in sleep labs. In one of those tests, three people were allowed to dream, and three were not. The first three were awakened after their dream, and the other three were awakened as they began their dream. The people who were allowed to dream experienced no changes in normal life, but those who were not allowed to dream for several days experienced personality disturbances, weight gain, and even depression.[27] The expert's conclusion was that people must dream!

Scientists also have discovered that the *continual* use of alcohol and drugs hinder and can even prohibit the dreaming process.[28] These people experience the same results as those who were not allowed to dream. Not being able to dream causes an even greater dependency on alcohol or drugs because these people cannot work through their situations during sleep. Please note that I am not referring to the occasional use of prescription drugs or a drink before dinner. This testing dealt with those who were considered addicted to alcohol or drugs. Taking an occasional sleeping pill or being on prescribed medicines will not shut down your dreaming process.

One of the most surprising results of study involves infants still in the womb. Dream experts have discovered that infants in the womb have the same sleep patterns as adults: shallow, dream, and deep sleep.[29] The Bible also gives us insight about infants in the womb. In Psalm 139, the psalmist said that God searched him and knew him, behind and before. In Jeremiah 1:5, we see that God knew Jeremiah before he was formed in his mother's womb. Before he came forth out of the womb, God had sanctified him and ordained him a prophet unto the nations. John the Baptist was supernaturally filled with the Holy Ghost while he was still in his mother's womb (Luke 1:41–44).

When people are grown, they may want to know their roots. Perhaps while infants are in the womb, the Lord gives them a glimpse of their *spiritual* roots, and they become God-conscious before they are even born. Then as they grow up, God-consciousness returns during sleep and through dreams. It's just a thought.

An interesting study was conducted by Dr. David Foulkes, professor of psychiatry at Emory University Medical School; he recorded the dreams of eight hundred children. The children slept in a sleep lab at the university nine nights per year over a five-year period. Children ages three and four had one- or two-sentence, simple dreams of playing or eating. The five- and six-year-olds also dreamed simple stories, but the dreams began to feature people they knew. The boys had more action in their dreams. Boys dreamed more of animals and conflict, and girls dreamed more about their dolls and family. Children seven and eight had more complex and personal dreams, which showed the desire to be an adult. There were fewer animals, less conflict, and more family members in the boys' dreams, and the girls began to act out more women's roles in their dreams. The dreams of nine to thirteen year olds had the same characteristics as adult dreams. The boys had more aggressive dreams, and the girls dreamed more of other girls as they played out girls' and women's roles. Overall, girls had more pleasant dreams than boys had. Children had only occasional nightmares. If a child was having recurring nightmares, something was happening during the day that the child was having difficulty coping with. The conclusion of this study is that through dreams children are prepared for adulthood.[30]

Parents, if your child is having repeated nightmares, check it out! These dreams don't automatically mean your child is being abused. Your child could be having difficulty adjusting at school. When our son, Jeff, was six, we moved to a different house. We fixed up his bedroom and put in bunk beds. He was the brave boy who wanted to sleep on the top bunk. Almost immediately, he began having nightmares. We could not figure out what was going on. After a while, I decided to make a change in his bedroom, and we made the bunk beds into twin beds. His nightmares immediately stopped. We then realized he had a fear of sleeping on the top bunk. He didn't tell us while he was awake, but the fear showed up in his sleep.

I encourage you to pray about your children's sleep. Ask them to share their dreams with you. You should evaluate their dreams and help them learn from their dreams. Dreams can help children, as well as adults, escape some of the pressures of life, act out their fears, and win! Through dreams, not only are children prepared for adulthood, but the Lord can make Himself known to them.

The Bible tells us that the child Samuel had an experience with God as he slept. As Samuel was laid down to sleep, the Lord called Samuel, and the young boy answered, "Here I am!" (see 1 Samuel 3:3–10). I have found that children are usually more open and sensitive to the Lord than adults are. Even some adults who have strayed from their Christian walk and have returned to their faith later in life share that they had some type of spiritual experience when they were children.

What Are Our Dreams Telling Us?

Overall both men's and women's dreams are similar in meaning and purpose, but the symbols have a male-female difference. In 1987, however, it was discovered that as sex roles are changing so are the dream patterns.[31]

Women used to dream mainly of being indoors in brightly decorated rooms. Now their dreams include outdoor scenes just as men's dreams do. Conversations in women's dreams used to be emotional. Now their dreams are more active. Women used to dream of being victims, but now they are the aggressors in their dreams. They identify people by occupation, a feature once typical only of men. Women used to dream of courtship, weddings, and marriage. Now their dreams include vivid bedroom scenes. Dreams do change according to the environment because dreams deal with current circumstances.

Circumstances you experience *during sleep* affect your dreams also. You may dream you are going to the bathroom, awake, and realize you already did. You may feel pain in a dream and find that you are in pain when you awake. Studies have found that a pregnant woman's dreams change during each new trimester.[32] Even the type of mattress or pillow you sleep on can affect your dreams.[33]

When people are depressed, they seem to sleep most of the time. Doctors say depression slows down the body and makes a person feel tired. I believe that's true, but I also think that God allows a depressed person to feel sleepy so that the person can work through his or her problems through the dreaming process. There are times when a doctor may prescribe drugs to help a person sleep, and that can be helpful. But if these prescribed drugs have a negative effect or become habitual, they could hinder the dreaming process and cause the person to need more time to recover.

The Effects of Tradition

Dreams are beneficial, yet many of the benefits have not been widely recognized. Our tradition has limited our thinking about the importance of dreams. Eastern tradition came from the Greek philosopher Plato, who lived from 427 to 347 B.C. He taught that we receive knowledge from three sources: our five senses, our mind, and our spirit. In fact, the authors of the Hindu scriptures *(Upanishads)* maintained that dreaming is a higher state of consciousness than waking. They encouraged individuals to seek their purpose in life through dreams. Asia, India, and the Eastern culture still hold to this concept.[34] I do not go that far in my teaching on dreams, but I do want to make you aware that some cultures put a high value on dreams.

Plato's student Aristotle lived from 384 to 322 B.C. Aristotle taught that man receives knowledge from only two sources: the five senses and the mind; he believed that we have no spirit. The ultimate humanist, he influenced today's Western culture, and our society has clung to his philosophy. Aristotle's humanistic influence is one of the reasons it took so long for American scientists to start studying dreams.[35]

How Important Are My Dreams?

Even though our society has been slow in recognizing the value of dreams, I believe that is getting ready to change. Dreams are for your benefit. It's good to know your real self will surface in your dreams. We all need to learn to face ourselves. Tired of paying high counseling fees? Your dreams can be free counselors. Dreams are truly a release from the day's frustrations as you work through your problems without the interference that you face when you are awake. Dreams can reveal truth and show you what will happen if you continue whatever you're doing. Dreams can warn and can give direction, correction, or peace. Dreams are truly concerned about you personally because those dreams come from you! Even nightmares can help you face difficult situations.[36]

Important discoveries have been made through dreams. Dreams can even bring forth physical healing. Most physicians agree that the mind has a powerful influence over the body. In the same way, dream experts have discovered that dreams also have an effect on the body. People have had dreams that are considered healing or intervention dreams, which point out problems or suggest treatments for sickness, and some of these dreams have come even before the symptoms of a disorder appear.[37] That certainly makes me want to become more aware of my dreams.

A Doctor's Thoughts on Dreams

In a recent interview, Dr. Bernie Siegel, a general and pediatric surgeon and author of the best-selling book *Love, Medicine, and Miracles,* explained his thoughts on dreams and how they can reflect insight into our illnesses and healing. "To me dreams represent what I call the universal language, how creation or God speaks to us through universal symbols. My true sense is that one of the reasons we sleep is to allow ourselves to be in touch with this inner wisdom and knowledge that present themselves to us through dreams." He continued, "While they're quiet, there's this other wisdom that comes forward. Here's one reason I call it a wisdom. There are people whose intellect tells them—don't have an operation or don't this, don't that, and they may make a decision that comes from their intellect. Again, it's their inner wisdom—intuitive wisdom, heart wisdom, whatever you want to call it—saying yes or no, this is good or not good for you. And believe me, that other wisdom knows more."[38]

Chapter 6

The Dark Speeches
of the Night

*And he said, Hear now my words: If there be a prophet among you,
I the Lord will make myself known unto him in a vision,
and will speak unto him in a dream.*

Numbers 12:6

God refers to dreams as "dark speeches" in Numbers 12. A dark speech is a hard question, proverb, or riddle that is given while a person is asleep; this speech that must be evaluated and interpreted. Scripture tells us that we can understand these dark speeches and that understanding comes through prayerful evaluation of our dreams (see Psalm 49:4; 78:2; Proverbs 1:6; Daniel 8:23).

God Speaks in the Night

The dreams recorded in the Bible give us a glimpse of how the Lord can reveal Himself to His people. The Bible assures us that God spoke to people through dreams and visions and even sent His angels to appear in dreams and to be seen in visions in order to give revelation and instruction. Even unbelievers in the Bible had dreams of significance, but for the most part, they needed men of God to interpret their dreams. Joseph and Daniel were men who saved their nation by interpreting the dreams of unbelieving kings. There were five dreams and three visions surrounding the birth of Christ. Abraham, Isaac, Jacob, Joseph, Isaiah, Daniel, Jeremiah, Peter, Paul, and John—just to name a few—were led and encouraged through God-given dreams. If we removed the dreams and visions from the Bible, we would have to tear out over one-third of it, including the whole of Revelation. Through dreams people foresaw future events, glimpsed into the spirit realm, and received direction, confirmation, consolation, and warning.

But does God still speak to people through their dreams today? Does God notice your circumstances enough to speak to you *personally* through a dream? While reading the following accounts of biblical dreams, you may realize that you have already had spiritual dreams but did not recognize them as such. The traditions of our day may have affected your thinking. Some people who have a supernatural experience may let it fade because they are not seeking after the heart of God. There are times when a concerned family member asks God to somehow speak to an unbelieving loved one, and God answers the prayer by revealing Himself through a dream or vision. But it is still up to the dreamer to acknowledge and respond to what he or she has seen.

May the cry of your heart be as mine: "Oh, Lord, make Yourself known to me even as You did to Your servants in Bible days."

Let's look at some biblical dreams. I won't try to examine them all, but I have listed them in the latter part of this chapter, in case you want to do a more in-depth study for yourself. I will refer to dreams and night visions interchangeably because the Bible does not clearly distinguish between them. Night visions come as a person is either going into or coming out of sleep. A well-known teacher made the statement that visions reveal God's nature, and dreams reveal God's will. Think about that statement as you continue to read. I'll discuss some of the people God spoke to in dreams, why He spoke to them, and the results of those dreams and night visions.

Dream Interpretations

There are four types of dream interpretations recorded in the Bible: the gift of interpretation, miraculous, false, and common sense.

Gift of Interpretation (Genesis 41:12; Daniel 1:17)

In my study, I have found only two men in the Bible—Joseph and Daniel—who were actually gifted by God to interpret dreams. These men did not seek the gift but sought God. It seems God knew these men would use this gift for His glory, not for their own glory. Even though Daniel's friends loved God and were faithful, they were not gifted in interpreting dreams. I do not believe there are many today who are gifted in dream interpretation due to a lack of teaching or a lack of seeking after God.

Miraculous Interpretation (Daniel 2:3–19)

A miraculous interpretation is the revealing of an unknown dream that only God could know; not even the person who had the dream remembers it. Even though I have helped many people understand their dreams, I have never experienced a miraculous interpretation. A biblical example of a miraculous interpretation is the story of King Nebuchadnezzar, who awoke from a troubling dream that he could not remember. When his wise men could not tell him his dream, he became so enraged that he decreed the slaughter of all the leaders. In terror, these leaders rushed to Daniel to tell him the terrible news. Daniel immediately called on his three friends to join with him in prayer. God then revealed to Daniel the king's dream and the interpretation of the dream in a night vision. God used a vision to reveal a dream—one supernatural to reveal another supernatural.

When Daniel told the king the dream, the king knew the interpretation was true. Daniel publicly gave the glory to God, saying, "He revealeth the deep and secret things" (Daniel 2:22).

The king agreed saying, "Of a truth it is, that your God is a God of gods, and a Lord of kings, and a revealer of secrets" (Daniel 2:47). God received the glory, Daniel received promotion, and all the leaders were spared!

False Interpretations (Numbers 12:6, Jeremiah 23:21–27 and Deuteronomy 13:3)

Although the Bible assures us that the Lord has His prophets through whom He speaks in dreams, it warns that people can claim that God has spoken to them in a dream when in reality He has not. The false prophets in biblical times were said to have prophesied lies (or exaggerated) from the deceit of their own hearts to build up themselves instead of God. They were not as Daniel, who wanted God to receive all the glory. God said He will forget and forsake those who speak lies.

Common Sense Interpretation (Judges 7:13–15)

Gideon provided an example of this type of interpretation when he overheard the Midianite interpret a soldier's symbolic dream. I'll talk about this dream in more detail later. But remember that God gave you common sense! Use it.

Biblical Dreamers

Abraham (Genesis 15:12)

God showed Abraham future events and confirmed His covenant with him *after Abraham had fallen into a deep sleep.* Perhaps Abraham was at a point in his life where it was difficult for him to comprehend God's overwhelming promises to him when he was awake. Therefore, God continued to speak to him when he was in deep sleep.

The first recorded warning dream came to Abimelech, a king who had taken Abraham's wife, Sarah, into his harem. To keep from being killed, Abraham had told a half-truth that Sarah was his sister. (She was his half sister.) In a dream, God warned Abimelech not to touch her. Upon awakening, Abimelech returned Sarah to Abraham and even blessed him with much wealth.

Jacob (Genesis 28; 31)

Jacob, the grandson of Abraham, had several experiences of God's mercy toward him through his dreams. Jacob was on the run from his brother Esau and fell asleep with a stone for his pillow in a field. That night he got a glimpse of that heavenly realm when he dreamed of a ladder that reached into heaven and that had angels ascending and descending on it. God stood above it, spoke to Jacob, and renewed the covenant of his grandfather Abraham. Jacob awoke and knew that God had spoken to him.

This dream had a profound effect on Jacob. He had been deceptive and had run away from his brother and, no doubt, from God. As a result of this dream, he named this wilderness Bethel, meaning House of God, and built an altar, where he worshipped God and made a vow and gave a tithe. This was the beginning of change for Jacob.

Perhaps you have never had such an impacting spiritual dream, but rest assured the Lord can minister to you. Then you, too, can call your wilderness Bethel, the place where you saw God.

Later in Jacob's life, after working for his father-in-law, Laban, for many years, God sent His angel to speak in a dream to let Jacob know it was time for him to return to his homeland. Due to strife with his father-in-law, Jacob had to sneak away. When Laban pursued Jacob, God used a dream to warn Laban not to speak to Jacob good or bad but to let him go. As a result of that dream, Laban and Jacob made a covenant.

Unlike Jacob, not every person who has heard from God through a dream or a night vision has been obedient, however. Even today people have dreams and remember them but do not listen to the message and take action. Yet dreams are not a waste of God's time, though people ignore them; they show God's mercy.

Balaam

There are several examples of those who had God-given dreams and did not heed the message. Balaam, a prophet of Israel, was hired by Balak, an enemy of Israel, to curse the nation (Numbers 22—25). God warned Balaam through a dream not to be a part of Balak's plan, but Balaam did not obey. Jude 10–13 says that Balaam, due to his greediness for the reward, brought a nation into error. Greed, the *love* of money, caused Balaam to disobey his God-given dreams. Balaam is still remembered as a traitor to his nation. God tried to warn him and help him, but he would not listen. Oh, that we would heed our dreams!

Daniel and King Nebuchadnezzar

In Daniel 4, we read of King Nebuchadnezzar's troubling symbolic dream that revealed his heart of pride. This dream so shook the king that he shared his dream with his trusted, godly servant Daniel. Daniel revealed the interpretation and called on the king to repent. For a while the king humbled himself, but after a year, he forgot the message of his dream and again rose up in pride. As a result, he was forced to eat in a field like an animal. His mind was finally restored only when he recognized the King of all kings. I wonder if we go through unnecessary circumstances because we do not realize that one of our dreams was a warning message.

Pilate (Matthew 27:19)

Pilate was another man who did not listen to a dream. He was struggling to know what to do with Jesus. His wife had a dream and sent a message to her husband saying, "Have thou nothing to do with that just man: for I have suffered many things this day in a dream because of him." But Pilate feared the people and did not listen to his wife or heed the warning of the dream. Somehow he thought he could just wash his hands of this man Jesus.

Joseph (Genesis 37)

Joseph, the seventeen-year-old son of Jacob, had two symbolic dreams that revealed the future to him. In the first dream, his family was binding sheaves in the field, and Joseph's sheaf stood upright while the others' sheaves bowed to his sheaf. In the next dream, the sun, moon, and eleven stars bowed to him. Even though these dreams were in symbols, the meaning was clearly understood. Joseph's father and his eleven brothers said to him, "Are you going to have dominion over us?" His brothers hated him for his dreams.

This situation shows that it is not always wise to share your dreams with others. In telling his dreams to his brothers, Joseph suffered much. I don't think Joseph realized what was going to happen to him or how many years it would take before his dreams would be fulfilled, but the dreams did come to pass. Because Joseph understood these dreams, years later he could say to his brothers with confidence that what they meant for evil God meant for good (Genesis 50:20).

Joseph, as a result of the God-given gift of dream interpretation, was able to save many nations. But he endured years of testing before he saw the result of his dreams. Many people want instant gratification. However, as with other areas of gifting, I have found that we will be tested to see if we will develop and use our gift for God's glory regardless of the circumstances.

Look at Joseph's testing. Dreams were an active part of his life. After being betrayed and sold into slavery by his brothers, he ended up in prison. And things got worse before they got better. In the depth of prison when he could have been in total self-pity, he was sensitive enough to interpret the symbolic dreams of his fellow prisoners—Pharaoh's chief butler and baker. They were depressed because there was no one who could interpret their dreams. Joseph's response was that interpretations belong to God. Even in the depth of prison, he was confident in God.

So the butler told of his dream of a vine with three branches that budded clusters of grapes, which he pressed into Pharaoh's cup. The baker dreamed of three white baskets in which were meats for Pharaoh, and birds ate out of the basket on his head. Within three days of Joseph's interpretation, the dreams came to pass; the butler was restored to his position, and the baker put to death (Genesis 40).

The dreams had dealt with their positions and their current situations and had shown their immediate future. (Take note that the baker's dream of death was symbolic.) Had these men not told their dreams to Joseph, the dreams would have, no doubt, come to pass anyway. But because God had a servant ready to interpret these dreams, God received the glory, and Joseph was eventually restored.

Joseph remained in prison after the butler was released, but two years later Pharaoh had two dreams that no one could interpret. Pharaoh was confident that his dreams were relevant to his nation's future and was furious that no one could interpret his dreams. It was then that the butler, who had been restored to his position and had promised to help Joseph, remembered Joseph's gift of dream interpretation.

When Joseph was called before Pharaoh, Joseph said that God alone would give Pharaoh the answer of peace. Joseph didn't let the position of Pharaoh intimidate him. Joseph gave all the credit to God! He passed another test!

Will you pass your test?

After Joseph interpreted the dreams of Pharaoh, Joseph said that the dreams had been doubled (meaning that the two dreams contained the same message) because the message was established by God, and God would shortly bring it to pass. Evidently, Joseph understood the purpose of doubled dreams because he had experienced the result of his own. Some people have repeating dreams, which may have different symbols but the same meaning, and they do not know to evaluate the dreams as one. You may want to take another look at some of your recurring dreams after reading about Joseph.

When you have a dream that shows the future, don't think the fulfillment should always happen immediately as with the butler and the baker. It took thirteen years for Joseph's teenage dreams to come to pass and fourteen years for Pharaoh's dreams to be fulfilled.

Notice that Pharaoh elevated Joseph to second-in-command *before the famine ever began!* The result of this interpretation was that Pharaoh acknowledged the God Joseph served, and Joseph was not only restored but also promoted to second-in-command; the nation of Egypt and many other nations were saved during the time of famine. To top it all off, Joseph and his family were eventually reunited, and the lineage of the Jews was perpetuated. God again fulfilled His plan by people being sensitive to their dreams.

Gideon (Judges 7:13–15)

Symbolic dreams can be understood! Gideon's army had been reduced to only three hundred men, and they were facing the massive Midianite army. Gideon called on the Lord, and the Lord told him that because he was afraid to fight, he should spy on the Midianite army. Then he would hear something that would strengthen him.

Gideon overheard two soldiers talking, and one soldier shared with a fellow soldier a dream about a "cake of barley bread that tumbled into the host of Midian, and came into a tent, and smote it that it fell, and overturned."

The soldier's friend immediately gave the interpretation: "This is nothing else save the sword of Gideon . . .

for into his hand hath God delivered Midian, and all the host."

That was enough for Gideon! He worshipped the Lord, returned to his small army, and said, "Arise; for the LORD hath delivered into your hand the host of Midian." Then Gideon's army of three hundred, with the help of the Lord, defeated the fierce Midianite army.

When you're in an overwhelming situation and feel, as Gideon, that you are outnumbered, call on the Lord and ask Him to give direction even as you sleep. Then when you awake, take time to remember your dream, meditate on it, evaluate your current situation, and see what the Lord has to say to you.

David (Psalm 17:3)

David understood the purpose of dreams, which can test the motives of our heart. He said that God proved his heart, visited him in the night, tried him, and found nothing; he had purposed that his mouth would not transgress. Not many of us can say, as David, that the Lord can find nothing wrong with us because we have carefully watched our words when we were awake. The point of this passage is that the night can be a time when God tests our heart's motives as we sleep; then we cannot argue, trying to defend ourselves to Him. He can visit us, make a deposit within us, and even refine and purge us as we sleep. We can awake refreshed and restored due to the changes that have taken place!

Solomon (1 Kings 3:3–15)

Solomon is another man whose heart was tested by God through a dream. When Solomon was a new king, he went to Gibeon to *worship and receive his strength from the Lord.* It was after worship that the Lord appeared to

81

him in a dream and said, "Ask what I shall give thee." That was a test question. Solomon was not awake, and God knew Solomon would answer him from his heart. God was pleased when Solomon replied, "Give therefore your servant an understanding heart to judge thy people, that I may discern between good and bad." God gave to Solomon such a wise heart that there was none like him. In addition to this wisdom, God also gave him wealth and honor.

When I became aware of the implications of this Scripture, that God gave Solomon wisdom through a dream, I saw even more significance of the night and dreams. If God can do that for Solomon, He can do that for me and for you! Ask yourself how you would respond if God came to you in your sleep and asked the same question He asked Solomon. I've often said that if the Lord were to appear to us in His glory while we were awake and ask that question, immediately our minds would start thinking, "I must give a spiritual answer; after all, this is the Lord!" Then we would try to give a response that would please Him: "Oh, Lord, I just want to be spiritual and follow You wherever You lead."

But when we are asleep, we will answer from the depth of our heart. A lonely single lady may ask for a husband and not be particular about his Christian qualifications. One in financial need may ask for money and not for the wisdom to get a promotion on the job. One having marital problems may ask for a new mate. One facing difficult circumstances may ask for the opportunity to move and not for the strength to face the circumstances. What if the Lord answers us according to our words in our sleep! Solomon had been in worship, and his heart was ready for God's question.

How ready are you?

In 2 Chronicles 7:14, God spoke to the heart of

Solomon in another dream, and thus God spoke to the heart of the nation.

> *If my people, which are called by my name,*
> *shall humble themselves, and pray, and seek my face,*
> *and turn from their wicked ways;*
> *then will I hear from heaven, and will forgive their sin,*
> *and will heal their land.*

Solomon received these godly instructions on how to have revival, and few Christians realize that this often-quoted verse was spoken by God to Solomon in a night vision. This powerful verse is still affecting people and nations today, and the message came through a dream in the night!

Daniel (Daniel 7)

There are symbolic dreams that require interpretation from someone other than the dreamer. Several of Daniel's dreams had to be interpreted by an angel. Daniel, a godly man who was taken into Babylonian captivity when he was a teenager, had symbolic dreams that showed future events for his time and prophetically for our day as well. Some of them so impacted Daniel that his spirit grieved for days. Through the years, he wrote down these dreams and visions, and they are still influencing lives today!

In chapter 7, Daniel shared one of his symbolic dreams, which revealed the future antichrist system through the symbols of four great beasts—the lion, the bear, the leopard, and the beast with iron teeth and ten horns. He also saw the Ancient of Days (God) who sat upon His throne. Daniel did not understand the dream and asked one who stood by him in the dream. This one in his dream may have been the angel Gabriel because Gabriel was later sent to bring understanding to Daniel's visions. If God sent an angel to Daniel to give him understanding, then surely He will help us when we have a God-given dream. If you have an impacting dream and do not understand it, do as Daniel did; call on the Lord for the interpretation. As Daniel said, "There is a God in heaven that revealeth secrets" (Daniel 2:28).

Jesus Christ

After evaluating some of the dreams of the Old Testament, let's look at some of the dreams of the New Testament. I've heard the Christmas story since I was a young child, but I never realized the important role that dreams and visions played in the birth of Christ. The three visions shared by Luke are of angelic visitations. In the first chapter of Luke, he detailed the vision of the angel Gabriel, who was sent to Zechariah. As Zechariah carried out his priestly duties, Gabriel suddenly appeared to tell him that he and his wife, Elizabeth, would have a son named John and that their son would be the forerunner of the Messiah. This was an answer to prayer for Zechariah. Next, Luke shared that Gabriel visited a young virgin named Mary who would be the mother of the Messiah. Then on the eve of the birth of Christ, a host of angels appeared to the shepherds in the field, bringing them good tidings of great joy. The importance and impact of these angelic visions cannot be denied. The five dreams that surround the birth of Christ are recorded in the Book of Matthew. These were dreams that gave direction and warning. Four out of the five dreams were to Joseph. In Matthew 1, an angel came to Joseph in a dream and told him that he was not to be afraid to take Mary as his wife because the child she was carrying was conceived by the Holy Ghost. Joseph could have easily felt that this dream was not from God but that it had come from his love and feelings of sympathy for Mary. But Joseph heeded the dream and it connected him to his destiny. The wise men who found the Christ child were warned not to return to King Herod, and they traveled home another way. When warned by another dream, Joseph fled to Egypt, protecting the Christ child. This dream came right before King Herod decreed to kill all the boys under two years old. Joseph did not return from Egypt with his family until he was given instruction through yet another dream. Joseph fulfilled prophecy when he moved to Nazareth as directed by God through a fourth dream, and Jesus was known as a Nazarene. It is evident that Joseph had learned to depend on his God-given dreams. It is also evident that God used these dreams to protect His Son.

Because dreams surrounded His birth, I thought Jesus would have said something about dreams. Whenever I study, I want to know what Jesus said, but I could not find that He said anything about the subject of dreams. At first, I was disheartened, but as I continued to study, I began to realize that Jesus did use the dream language through his teaching of the parables. Jesus tested the hearts of the people while they were awake in the same way that dreams tested their hearts while they were asleep. I began to see that parables are symbolic stories like dreams are. It seems parables and dreams have the same purpose. The Greek words for parable are *parabole,* meaning symbols of fictitious narrative of common life conveying a moral, and *paroimiah,* meaning to go alongside of. It's interesting to me that the meaning of parable is very similar to the meaning of Holy Spirit Comforter, which means one called alongside of—*paracletos* (John 16:7–15). The Holy Spirit comes alongside to comfort, and parables come alongside to give meaning to everyday life.

The significance of parables is made obvious by the

large number of them that were recorded. Parables are stories that go alongside common life and convey moral values. Jesus used common things to penetrate people's hearts—trees, wheat, salt, light, treasures, fowls, lilies, dogs, swine, fruit, foundations, bridegrooms and brides, candles, cloth, corn, birds, children, and many more. These parables had a dual purpose; they gave practical wisdom and revealed spiritual mysteries, which tested the hearts of those who listened. Some of these parables really upset the religious leaders; in fact, there were times when they wanted to kill Jesus because of His parables! Jesus spoke so many parables that the disciples finally came to Him and asked why he so often used parables. His answer really caught them off guard. He told them that it was given to them to understand the mysteries of the kingdom of heaven but not to some others. There must have been shocked and puzzled expressions on the disciples' faces after Jesus made this statement. They were probably wondering if Jesus realized that they didn't understand the parables either. Jesus then said that the people could not understand the messages of these parables due to the hardness of their hearts, which caused their spiritual ears to become dull. They had become so insensitive and rebellious that they could not be converted or healed. Jesus then shared the purpose of the parables with His disciples. The parables revealed the condition of the people's hearts. He said that if they would hear the principle of the parable, they would be healed. If they refused to listen with their hearts, they would continue in their rebellion and lose the blessing the parable was revealing to them.

I think there's a reason why Jesus used parables instead of dreams. When He was here on earth, He was in the flesh and was limited in space; He could not be everywhere at once. Jesus spoke with parables that revealed and tested the motives of those around him while they were awake. Today, He is not limited by space because the Holy Spirit has come. Therefore, He can speak to our spirit man by His Spirit through His Word and His ministers when we are awake and through our dreams—the language of the Spirit—when we are asleep.

The Holy Spirit

Dreams can minister to us in the same way that the Holy Spirit ministers to us. If the Holy Spirit has come to minister to us always, the night and sleep are included (John 16:7–15). Note the similarities between the purpose of the Holy Spirit and the purpose of dreams:

- The Holy Spirit comforts; dreams refresh.
- The Holy Spirit convicts; dreams reveal blind spots.
- The Holy Spirit guides; dreams give direction and help solve problems.
- The Holy Spirit reveals; dreams show us things to come.
- The Holy Spirit leads us into truth; dreams show us our true selves.

I've had several people share their testimony with me and say that they received the baptism of the Holy Spirit in their sleep. They had been *seeking* to be filled with the Spirit, had become discouraged, and went home to "sleep on it." They awoke speaking in that heavenly language.

The purpose of our dreams in the night may go deeper than any of us realize. Jesus said it was expedient *for you* that He go away so the Holy Spirit Comforter could come. And the Comforter is with us

87

always—twenty-four hours a day—working in us when we are awake and when we are asleep. The New Testament is filled with supernatural experiences. I encourage you to study them for yourself.

A List of Biblical Dreams

To help you in your further study of biblical dreams, I have listed them below.

- Concerning Sarah and Abraham (Genesis 20:3–6)
- Revealing the spirit realm to Jacob (Genesis 28:12)
- Giving direction to Jacob (Genesis 31:10–13)
- Warning Laban (Genesis 31:24)
- Revealing the future to Joseph (Genesis 37:5)
- Revealing the future to the chief butler (Genesis 40:5)
- Revealing the future to the chief baker (Genesis 40:5)
- Revealing to Pharaoh the famine to come (Genesis 41:7)
- Directing Jacob to go to Egypt (Genesis 46:2)
- Revealing Gideon's future victory (Judges 7:13)
- Testing Solomon's heart (1 Kings 3:5)
- Giving Solomon principles for revival (1 Kings 9:1)
- Revealing the spirit realm to Eliphaz (Job 4:13)
- Revealing Job's fear (Job 7:14)
- Revealing the future of King Nebuchadnezzar (Daniel 2:3)

- Warning King Nebuchadnezzar (Daniel 4:5)
- Revealing the future to Daniel (Daniel 7:1)
- Revealing more of the future to Daniel (Daniel 8:1)
- Revealing the spirit realm to Daniel (Daniel 10:5)
- Showing false prophets (Jeremiah 23:27–32, 29:8; Zechariah 10:2)
- Giving direction to Joseph (Matthew 1:20)
- Warning the wise men to return home another way (Matthew 2:12)
- Warning Joseph to flee to Egypt (Matthew 2:13)
- Directing Joseph to return home (Matthew 2:19)
- Warning Joseph of King Herod (Matthew 2:22)
- Warning Pilate's wife (Matthew 27:19)
- Revealing the spirit realm to Cornelius (Acts 10:3)
- Revealing the spirit realm to Peter (Acts 10:10)
- Giving Paul direction (Acts 16:9)
- Telling Paul to bear witness in Rome (Acts 23:11)
- Directing Paul to safety (Acts 27:23–24)
- Revealing the spirit realm to John (Revelation 1:10–17)

Chapter 7

Understanding and Interpreting Your Dreams

*And they said unto him, We have dreamed a dream,
and there is no interpreter of it.
And Joseph said unto them,
Do not interpretations belong to God?*

Genesis 40:8

One way to attend your own funeral and still live to tell about it is to dream about it. Years ago when we first began to take our dreams seriously, Fred dreamed that he attended his own funeral. In his dream, there were preachers from our former denomination, and one of the top officials, a man in whom Fred had great confidence, preached at the funeral. After the funeral, Fred stood in the viewing line, listening to other people comment about him, until it was his turn to look in the casket. When he looked in the casket, he saw himself in it. He then awoke.

When he told me about this dream, we laughed. He described how peaceful he seemed in the casket. We were actually joking around about the dream when, almost as an afterthought, I said that we should evaluate it. As we began to go step-by-step through his dream, he began to realize that the dream showed that certain legalistic traditions that had been formed in him were now dying out. This had not been a silly dream but a revealing one. As we continued to talk about the dream, the presence of the Lord began to overwhelm us, confirming that revelation. If Fred had not shared his dream with me, he probably would have forgotten it. God

90

would still work in him if the dream were forgotten, but the value of the dream was in knowing that the Lord was *continuing* to work in him. No matter how silly or scary you feel your dreams may seem, take the time to evaluate them. I believe that you, too, will see the continuing work of the Lord in your life.

First Things First

What do our dreams mean anyway? Through the ages, men and women have asked this question. There have always been other men and women to offer their interpretations. As dream research moves into the laboratory, some of the country's leading scientists are working to unravel the mysteries of those symbols and images that appear in our head while we are asleep. Like dream interpreters of old, these scientists frequently do not agree with each other. Scientists do agree that dreams are important and, for the most part, agree that the dreamer can evaluate and interpret his or her dream.[39]

Yes, dreams can give guidance, and we should evaluate them. Remember, however, that dreams are only one of the tools given to us to help us. People who seek spiritual experiences without seeking the God of the experience will end up in confusion. King Saul is an example of such a person; he sought guidance from prophets and dreams, and when he did not get the answers he wanted, he sought the counsel of a witch (1 Samuel 28:7). There is a similar phenomenon today. Advertising on TV lures people to seek direction through the counsel of psychics. Millions of dollars are spent on the psychic hotlines. Realize that if you need help through dreams, God knows how to get in touch with you. When you seek Him first and foremost in your life, your dreams will come naturally, even supernaturally.

How Can I Remember My Dreams?

Before you can understand and interpret your dreams, you have to remember them. The following ideas may give you some help in remembering your dreams. Before going to sleep, prepare the atmosphere with soft music (not TV news), pray over your sleep, claim the sleeper's promise of Psalm 127:2 of blessings in sleep, meditate on the answers that you need, and repeat quietly as you doze off, "I will remember my dream and receive the answers that I need." Disturbances such as a loud alarm clock can jar the memory of your dream from you. In fact, dreams fade fast, often within ten minutes of waking, so keep a pad of paper and a pen next to your bed so you can write down the dreams you remember; then you won't forget, exaggerate, or change them when you tell them. When you get into this habit, remembering your dreams will not be difficult.

While you awake slowly and meditate on the thoughts you were having as you awoke, keep your eyes closed for a few minutes (don't go back to sleep) and allow that dream to unfold again before you. After writing down your dream, read and analyze it briefly. It may seem disjointed, but as you think about the dream during the day, more understanding will come to you. Later in the day, when you have the opportunity, read it again and evaluate your dream in light of your current circumstances, looking for the principles of the dream. Ask questions about your dream and relate it to what is currently happening in your life. Scientists have discovered the dream that awakens you is probably the most important dream you've had that night.[40]

Can I Understand and Interpret My Dreams?

You are the most qualified person to interpret your dreams. It's your dream, not someone else's. Whenever I've helped a person who is struggling to interpret a difficult dream, I've found that several things are usually causing the difficulty. The person did not relate the dream to his or her current situation, did not evaluate the symbols in the dream correctly, or did not recognize the principle of the dream. A simple, overlooked *key* can unlock the meaning of a dream.

When you evaluate your dream, do not strain for the interpretation because this may cause you to exaggerate. The length of the dream does not matter. It is the message (principle) of the dream that counts. Do not try to *over-spiritualize* your dream. Use your common sense by examining your current situation and by evaluating the series of pictures and events in your dream. Ask relevant questions. Usually the interpretation is obvious if you take time to evaluate your dream. Once you have understanding, interpreting your dreams will become routine. The next step will be to heed your dreams.

I'm going to give you a list of questions to ask about your dreams. After you have gone through this list, I believe you will have greater understanding of how to interpret your dreams. Just remember to keep the interpretation simple, personal, and honest.

Simple

Ask simple, common sense questions about the people, animals, places, or things that were in your dream. What is your impression of what was going on? What does the person, animal, place, or thing in your dream represent to you? What were the facial expressions? What was happening in this dream that is happening in your own life? What could your inner man be trying to tell you about solving any problems you have in your current situation? What is the principle of the dream? Does it represent fear, the future, the past, or the present? Remember that dreams can become nightmares if they are not dealt with.

Personal

Keep the interpretation personal. What does the dream really mean to you? Another person's opinion may take you off in a different direction.

Honest

Keep the interpretation honest. Is your hidden self being revealed? Are you in a spiritual struggle on the inside? Remember, repetitive dreams can represent areas in your life that you are not willing to face during your waking hours, or these dreams could represent what is called a *blind spot* in your life, something to which you are oblivious. Face yourself! It'll do you good. Once you face your situation, repetitive dreams should cease.

Testing Your Dreams

Dream experts say we can test a dream through our feelings.[41] When you wake up, analyze your feelings. Were you elated? Anxious? Depressed? Even if you do not remember your dream, your mood is a clear indication of what was going on inside you. Unpleasant feelings suggest that you should pay attention to *yourself* to find out what is troubling you. A happy feeling needs no interpretation and is a wonderful way to start your day. When you awake refreshed, even if you don't remember your dream, thank the Lord for a good night.

If you have had a dream that gives direction and that affects others, pray for a confirmation if you feel you need one. An example is a dream that tells you to move. A move may affect you and your family. Talk to your mate before taking any action. For in the mouth of two or three witnesses every word may be established (Matthew 18:16).

If your dream has shown you a future event, it should come to pass. If it doesn't, put the dream on the shelf. Do not try to force a dream to become a reality. Doing so will only add to your stress. On the other hand, if you know your dream is giving correction or direction and it has been confirmed, heed the message. Do not ignore it and let the dream slip away. Be willing to be corrected if need be. Then take the action necessary.

Analyzing the Symbols of Your Dreams

You need to realize that no single interpretation of any one symbol will hold true for every dream. The important thing is what the symbol means to you personally.

The interpretation of your dream should confirm something in your spirit; there should be a sense of relief or a *yes* on the inside. Your dreams, whether you consider them natural or spiritual, should edify you.

There are symbols that frequently have the same meaning in everyone's dreams. Take the symbol of *water* in a dream as an example. You may dream of swimming in the water, enjoying yourself, and encouraging others to join you. At another time, you may see yourself drowning in water or drinking water. The symbol of water in a dream can represent the source of life, and knowing the symbolism can help you evaluate your dream. It's not just the water that is important in your dream; it's what you did in or with the water and what the interpretation means to you.

The following list of symbols has come from various dream experts who, through helping others walk through their dreams, have found a common thread (symbols) in dreams. Knowing the meaning of these symbols can be of value to you. Notice that these represent *natural* dream symbols, not spiritual, although I have found that these symbols can be of benefit for both natural and spiritual dream interpretations.

Symbol	Represents
Bus or van	Crowds, feeling peer pressure
Dust	Confusion
House	Your view of yourself
Car	Transportation or male ego
Travel	Your life's journey
Treasures	Ego
Money	Energy
Clothes	Inner feelings
Circles	Wholeness

Water	Source of life
Lower floor of tall building	Physical condition
Upper floor of tall building	Mental state
Basement	Inner man or the spirit of man
Sex	Thoughts of committing adultery or balancing masculine and feminine natures
Wars or battles	Battle on the inside
Falling	Helplessness, not on solid ground psychologically, insecurity, or lost footing
Falling myth	That you will die in real life if you hit the ground
Losing money or keys	Desire to throw away restraints, not wanting to grow up or take responsibility, or fear of losing power
Holding on to a ledge	Barely hanging on to a bit of growth
Being on stage and forgetting your lines	Fear of success
Missing boat, plane, etc.	Feeling you are missing out
Someone else driving you around	Without control of your life
Getting lost	Fear of disappearing because needs are not met or feeling unnecessary to others (The elderly frequently dream this.)
Flying	Escaping real life

Feeling paralyzed	Desire to avoid danger or awaking from a dream
Being pursued and unable to run away	Fear of your own wild impulses or feeling guilty about something and attempting to flee
Being naked	Fear that part of you that you want to keep concealed is showing or desire to release inhibitions and be a child again
Taking a test	Facing a real life test
Being late	Facing an unreachable goal
Losing teeth	Losing your grip on a situation or fear of losing your good appearance
Failing an exam	Feeling unprepared for life's demands or feeling success is too much to handle

Animal Symbol	**Represents**
Charging animals	Emotions, aggressive or fearful
Birds	Thoughts, ideas, or spiritual beings (such as eagles or doves)
Snakes	Sexual intercourse, fears, or phobias
Lion	Courage
House pet	Affection
Other animals	Emotions or creative expression

Color Symbols	**Represents**
Red	Anger or passion
White	Purity

Black	Fear or depression
Blue or green	Spirituality

People Symbols	**Represents**
Police or judge	Authority (parents, church, conscience)
King or president	Leadership qualities in yourself
Criminals or liars	Bad part of yourself or part out of balance
Shadows	Undeveloped areas of your life
Babies	New areas of growth
A famous person	A positive or negative trait in yourself (according to your thoughts of that person)
Other people	Disguised traits of yourself or of those close to you

Death Symbols	**Represents**
Dying	Part of you dying (bad habits), good quality dying (one you've ignored), or self-ego dying

Note: Physical death in a dream is usually symbolic.

Time Symbols	**Represents**
Time of day	A stage in your life
Dawn	Youth
Midday	Mid-life
Night	Declining years

Setting Symbol	**Represents**
Outdoors	Alienation or freedom and adventure

Action Symbol	Represents
Actions performed against you	Guilty or negative feelings about yourself that you prefer not to acknowledge
Actions you perform	What you want to perform in life but don't

Repeated Dreams Symbol	Represents
Three or more repeated dreams	Areas of importance you do not face while awake

A Further Examination of Dream Symbols

It is difficult to decide on which symbols to elaborate. I've had and heard of so many dynamic dreams that it would take volumes of books to explain them all. Due to this limited space, I will comment on only a few of the dream symbols, and I trust that these I have chosen will benefit you.

Animals

A man told me that he dreamed of a rhino, and when he awoke, he realized the animal represented the extra weight he had gained. Running or hiding from an animal in a dream usually represents running or hiding from a fearful situation when you are awake. Regardless of the type of animal in the dream, look for the principle represented.

Buildings

When I dream of being in a multi-level building, I notice which floor I am on. Recently, a young man came to me distraught over a dream. His entire dream had taken place in a basement. In the dream, he was fighting with terrible monsters. When I said that a basement usually represents the inner man or the spirit realm, he looked shocked.

"I'm a backslider," he confessed. "I'm in a battle for my life—just as that dream showed."

I then asked what he planned to do. His answer surprised me: "I'm not sure. I know I need to give my life to the Lord, but I can't right now."

He allowed me to pray for him, but he wouldn't pray for himself. My heart went out to him as he left, but I could not force him to make a right decision. A couple years later, I received a call from this man that he finally had given his life to the Lord and the nightmares had stopped.

Houses

The condition of the house is important. I often ask people, "How do you feel about yourself? Do you feel the condition of this house mirrors your condition?" If people have a poor self-image or an incorrect view of themselves (revealed by a run-down house in a dream), this view can change through the dreaming process.

Falling

This is the myth that you will die if you hit the ground when you fall in a dream. I've hit and gone through the ground several times in my dreams, and I'm still here to tell about it. If you consistently dream of falling, take a closer look at your current circumstances. Falling in dreams can reveal your feelings of helplessness.

Someone driving you around

Note who is driving and ask yourself what this person represents. Is the car in your dream a rusty Cadillac or a Lincoln Continental? A young minister visiting our church a while ago asked about a dream that had been bothering him. In the dream he was driving a rusty Cadillac, and he was following a new, sleek Lincoln Continental in which a well-known minister was riding. I told him that cars in dreams usually represent the male ego, and I asked him how he felt about himself. He looked at me, dropped his head, and said, "I feel like that rusty Cadillac. I do feel I'm worthwhile, but it hasn't come forth yet."

I then asked, "How do you feel about that minister?"

He broke into a smile and said, "He's my ideal! He's so successful in ministry he should be riding in a Continental." After this response, he realized what his dream meant. Later, he told me that dream was a turning point in his life.

My daughter was struggling with the decision of whether or not to get married when she had a dream about a car. In the dream, the young man came to pick her up in a beautiful, shiny, red Corvette. When he opened the door, the car was so filled with litter that she could not fit inside. She awoke knowing what to do. She is thankful to this day for that dream.

Sex

Sex in a dream can represent the thought of committing adultery, especially if you are struggling with lust and daydreaming about someone during the day. But for the most part, dream experts say that sex in a dream represents the balancing of the feminine and masculine natures within us.[42] All of us have feminine and masculine natures within; Eve was taken from Adam and was called woman, meaning *wombed* man. Although men and women are different in many ways, they are still alike in other ways, and we can get out of balance in our natures. Through the dreaming process, internal feminine and masculine natures can become balanced.

Death

Although there have been times when someone has dreamed about the death of a loved one and that loved one has died, this is not the rule. Dream experts say that death in a dream usually represents a part of you (a good habit or a good quality that is being ignored, or even your self-ego) that is dying out.[43] Don't panic when you dream of death, but evaluate what the death may represent to you. Remember Fred's dream of attending his own funeral? His dream revealed that the Lord was working in him.

What if I Cannot Understand My Dreams?

Sometimes the meaning of a dream seems to escape us. If you cannot understand your dream after evaluating, meditating on, and even praying over it, share it with someone in whom you have confidence. Choose someone who knows you well, a person with a proven godly lifestyle.

Can I Help Others Understand Their Dreams?

If you learn to understand your own dreams and want to help others, go for it. If you're good, expect to spend a lot of time listening to other people's dreams. Sometimes it can be a challenge to work with people because their dreams reveal their heart and their true motives. Be a coach and not a judge! If people come to you for an interpretation, ask questions about their current situation and about what the symbols mean to them. Then share any recognizable symbol (listed in this chapter). Remember that symbols mean different things to different people. For example, another person's culture can cause a particular symbol to have a different meaning. After I explain the symbols, people usually can interpret their own dream.

If people come to you for help interpreting their dreams, be honest. First of all, if you're new at interpreting dreams, tell the person. Of course, you'll find that some dreams are simple to understand—like that of the Midianite soldier. For other dreams, just a couple of comments can bring clarity—especially once you know the list of symbols.

Not everyone qualifies to interpret other people's dreams. This ministry, like others, takes time, experience, and preparation. Some dream experts say that interpretation takes about five years to learn.[44] The Bible says study to show yourself approved. As you study and learn to interpret dreams, realize the interpretation belongs to God. Give Him the credit. Do not become proud. There have been times when I had no understanding of a person's dream, and after we joined hands in prayer, the interpretation came. It wasn't me; it was from the Lord.

I don't want to make this so difficult that you never try to help anyone understand his or her dreams when you are asked. If you have a desire to study about dreams and learn to interpret your own, you will find that it does become easier, and the door will begin to open for you to help others.

Dream experts recommend that you know the person before attempting to interpret his or her dream. It may be difficult to be honest with someone you know well, but honesty is what the person needs. I've found it's best to use the symbol guide list and try to not get too personal. Let the symbols speak for themselves. Never impose your own interpretation on someone else. Ask people what the dream or symbols mean to them.

Experts tell us to never attempt hasty interpretations or interpretations by mail or over the phone. Doing so can get you into trouble. If you feel you can help the person, then share the symbols of natural dreams and allow the person to judge the meaning. Encourage people to study about dreams for themselves.

What if Someone I Know Appears in My Dream?

There are times when someone you know is an active part in or the main feature of your dream. Don't automatically think your dream is for the other person. Remember that 95 percent of our dreams are for us personally. Therefore, even if someone else is in your dream, the dream is more than likely for you alone.

I've had a few dreams I felt were for others, but I'm very cautious about sharing these dreams. When I do share, I usually get a good response. A few times I have

105

received a blank stare. I never put any pressure on people. I just tell them to shelve the dream if they do not feel it is for them. Then I slip away quietly.

A few years ago, I dreamed that I was at a large convention, and a nationally known female speaker was ministering there. Fred and I were sitting in the front row. The atmosphere was electrifying as the evangelist prayed for people, and many healings took place.

Suddenly, she asked me to come to the platform to minister with her as she prayed for the sick. I was shocked and thrilled at the same time. I stood up quickly, but when I glanced down and straightened my clothes, I realized that I was not properly dressed. I wore a beautiful jacket, but I had jeans with holes in them; I was mortified. Fred pushed me forward as I tried to tell him that I couldn't go. Eventually, I stumbled to the stage and tried to hide myself behind the evangelist. She kept looking back at me with confusion in her eyes and kept urging me to stand beside her. I remember feeling such embarrassment.

I knew my dream was trying to tell me something important, but I did not have the full interpretation. As I prayed over it, I sensed that my clothing represented the armor of God. I then read Ephesians 6 to get some understanding, and it tells us to have our loins girded about with truth. Still the full meaning just did not come to me.

A few days later, I casually mentioned this dream to my son, Jeff, because it was still bugging me. He meditated for a minute and then said, "I'm not sure what it means, Mom, but at Bible school when we studied the armor of God, we were taught that the belt of truth covered the loins and that the loins represented the emotions."

Suddenly, I knew the dream's meaning. The apostle Peter said to "gird up the loins [emotions] of your mind." The Lord (through my subconscious) was letting me know that if I wanted to go further in ministry, my emotions needed to "pull together." That revelation was a turning point in my life.

I said all that to say this. Another person was an active part of my dream (the woman evangelist), but my dream was not for her; it was for me.

There are few recordings of dreams in the Bible that were for others. Nathan, a proven man of God and a prophet, had visions and dreams that gave direction to King David, and David acknowledged that Nathan's words were for him (2 Samuel 7). Pilate's wife had a dream for her husband. I have a feeling that she had words with Pilate after he did not heed her dream about Jesus (Matthew 27:19).

If you feel you've had a dream for someone else, look at it objectively. Ask yourself if God could be calling you to pray for that person, not to reveal the dream to that person. God could be calling you to help the person in some way. The dream could be revealing your feelings about that person.

If you sense you need to share your dream, pray about *how* and *when*. Don't indicate that the dream is absolutely for the other person. If it isn't, you may be projecting your own problems on someone else! Don't be condemning. After you share your dream, ask, "Does this dream mean anything to you?" Don't ask the person to tell you how it relates to him or her. Be sure to allow people the right to judge for themselves whether or not the dream is for them. It should be confirmed in their spirit. If it isn't, tell people to put the dream on the shelf. After sharing your dream, if the person does not feel your dream relates, do not take it personally. Maybe it really wasn't for that person but just for you. Learn from your experience.

I caution you. If you do not really understand your own dreams, ask yourself why God would give you a dream for someone else. I'm not saying you won't ever have a dream for someone else; I'm telling you to carefully evaluate dreams you think may be for another person.

Avoiding False Dreams and Visions

With the New Age era and the various religions that now abound, we must become aware that Satan can promote a perverted view of dreams or visions. There are religions that have been based upon false dreams, fantasies, hallucinations, and trances. Most cults are built on private revelation apart from the Bible. Through these false dreams or visions, people have been drawn away from God and into deception and eventually damnation.

When your heart is turned toward the Lord, you do not have to fear your dreams. It is knowing the truth that makes you free. You will have understanding and be able to interpret your God-given dreams.

Chapter 8

The Profound Effects of Dreams and Visions

For God speaketh once, yea twice, yet man perceiveth it not.
In a dream, in a vision of the night,
when deep sleep falleth upon men, in slumberings upon the bed:
then he openeth the ears of men, and sealeth their instruction.

Job 33:14–16

The effects of the dreams in the Bible were life changing, and they still can impact our lives today. Through my dreams, I have had several paradigm shifts. One of my sons was healed through a song in his sleep, and another son was called to the ministry through a dream. My daughter received direction for her life in a dream, and my husband has had such penetrating dreams that he should probably be writing this book. Almost everywhere I go people who have heard this teaching come to me with a testimony of how their lives were changed when they began to realize they were not weird because they remembered their dreams and took them seriously.

Revelation of the Spirit Realm through Dreams

Numerous people whom I consider upstanding, God-fearing people have told me of supernatural visitations through their dreams that left them in awe and with new strength, peace, or encouragement. I've also had several

dreams in which I saw into or visited the spirit realm—
some in which my loved ones who have passed away
appeared to me. I don't think these dreams came to me
so that I would experience giant Holy Ghost goose
bumps or so that I could prove how spiritual I was. A
message that the afterlife is a reality seemed to linger
after these dreams, and I was always left with a desire to
draw closer to the Lord.

Could those who have passed from this earthly life
become a part of that great cloud of witnesses referred
to in Hebrews 12? Do these witnesses surround us to
encourage us in our earthly race until we meet again
over there? Is it possible that there are times when one
of those witnesses could be made known to us? I'm not
trying to be New Age, super spiritual, or weird, but the
Bible does say that we can entertain angels unaware. If
that can happen while we are awake, could it not also
happen in our sleep as revelation comes through our
dreams?

Revelation of the spirit realm through dreams is possible. One of the most shaking dreams I've had involv-
ing the revealing of the spirit realm happened during
one of our church revivals. During the first week of the
meeting, I was excited and encouraged. It was going so
well that we decided to extend it. In the beginning of the
second week, the meetings took a turn for the worse in
my opinion. The evangelist seemed to step on everyone's toes, including mine, and I got offended. When I
asked Fred to say something to him, he told me to pray
about it. Halfway through that second week, I left one of
the services so upset that I drove home and went straight
to bed. Totally frustrated, I cried out, "Lord, you've got
to do something about that evangelist!" I fussed and
fumed in my mind until I fell asleep and began to dream.

My dream started out so wonderfully. I dreamed I
was with a group of people in a beautiful, flower-filled

field, and the evangelist was leading us as we danced through the field together. Picture one of those television commercials in which everyone holds hands, laughs, skips, and twirls in slow motion across a field. I was enjoying myself until a lady interrupted us and said, "You don't know what happens when this evangelist preaches."

I responded, "Sure I do. Look what a fun time we're having." She then began to pull me away and told me to follow her. I didn't want to go, but it seemed I had no choice.

As we walked away, we began to go down into a smoke-filled cave, and we entered a long, dark tunnel with glass on either side of it. Fear gripped my heart because I realized we were entering hell. The place was smoky and hot, and I could smell something burning. As we were walking through the tunnel, I began to peer into the glass, and I could see anguished people whirling around in the smoke. Often their tormented faces would smash up against the glass, and I could see the terror in their eyes. I began to shout, "Get me out of here!"

Again the lady said to me, "You don't know what happens when the evangelist preaches."

I then saw a light at the end of the tunnel and ran for it. Upon leaving the tunnel, I was partially blinded by the light. We had entered a large Roman-style coliseum, and I felt my way to a seat. The lady sat beside me. As my vision cleared, I saw that activities were taking place. I saw a woman with a whip in her hand enter the stage. A young man who had been severely beaten stood beside her. They both seemed filled with terror. Then I heard a voice cry out, "Beat your son."

She sobbed and screamed, "I can't, I can't, I can't do it anymore!"

But as she said this, she hit her son, and he screamed as loudly as she did. Eventually, he collapsed and begged to die. Those in the arena began to mock him and chant, "You will never die."

It was horrible. As I looked around me, I was in terror as I realized that those mocking him were not people; they looked like demonic beings. In panic, I looked to see if the lady was still sitting next to me. She looked me straight in the eyes and again said, "You don't know what happens when this evangelist preaches."

I then heard a loud noise, and my eyes turned again toward the stage. The lady and her son were being dragged away, and another young man entered staggering. They tortured him, too, as he screamed for death. Again the crowd roared, "You will never die!"

Suddenly, the crowd and the young man looked up; I turned my eyes upward, too, and saw a huge container of what seemed to be boiling oil about to pour over this young man. I began to scream as the crowd of demonic beings roared. Again I heard, "You don't know what happens when this evangelist preaches."

I awoke crying and shaking, and those words were ringing in my ears: "You don't know what happens when this evangelist preaches." I could still smell the smoke. I was so alarmed that I practically fell out of my bed and went to another room.

Falling on my knees, I cried out to the Lord, "What does this dream mean?"

The Lord ministered to me as I wept before Him. That dream had shown me the awfulness of hell, but also it was as a mirror revealing the real me. God let me see my judgmental attitude toward the evangelist. I hadn't liked his style of preaching; I wanted everything to be my way. God revealed that this man was an evangelist and a prophet who had been sent to warn, correct, and stir up; I was reminded not to touch God's anointed. The Lord had not called the evangelist to entertain but to preach the Word so that people could be pulled from hell, the very place I had experienced that night. I continued to weep and repented before God.

The next morning, I called the evangelist and asked him to meet with me in my office. He sensed the urgency in my voice. When he arrived, I told him about my dream and asked him to forgive me, which he did, of course. He then shared with me that he felt I had literally visited hell that night, explaining why I could still smell the smoke when I awoke. We prayed together and prayed for the revival. I came to the meeting that night with a completely different attitude. The meeting was one of the greatest revivals our church had ever experienced. Many gave their hearts to Christ and were pulled from hell!

Dreams: Seeing through the Glass Darkly

That dream so affected my life that I will never forget it, and I don't want to forget it. That dream not only allowed me to see into the spirit realm but also allowed me to see inside myself. As I was thinking about the revelation of that dream, I was reminded of the "love chapter," 1 Corinthians 13, in which the apostle Paul said, "We see through a glass darkly; but then face to face."

In this reference, *glass* actually means to mirror—to look into, to see a reflection, to gaze intensely at something remarkable, and to look through. If you've ever looked into dark glass, you know that there are times when you can see your own reflection. The dark glass can act as a mirror. Some modern designers now use a type of mirrored glass on the outside of their commercial buildings. When you are walking by such a building and look at it, you see yourself; it's as if you were look-ing into a mirror. The person on the other side of the glass, however, can see through the glass to the outside. If the person on the inside of the building turns on an inside light, then the glass no longer reflects as a mirror; it becomes a window, and you can see inside.

Dreams have this same effect. When we are dream-ing, there are times when our dream is as a dark glass that becomes a mirror, and we gaze at our real selves. But dreams can go beyond that. There can be times when a light comes on behind the dark glass of our dreams, and we see into the spirit realm. We can look through the dark glass or beyond the mirror because Someone on the other side of that dark glass has turned on the light! However, we may not have a complete or clear understanding of what we have seen, and it can be as a riddle (dark speech) for a season.

Here's another example. In our church there are two mothers' nurseries, one on either side of our sanctuary. Dark, mirrored glass was installed in front of each of these nurseries so that the mothers can see out into the auditorium, but those on the outside cannot see into the nursery. If you look at the glass from the outside, you'll only see your own reflection; the glass acts as a mirror. But if one of the mothers on the inside of the nursery turns on a light, you can see inside. Previously, you may not have even realized there was a nursery behind that mirror.

At times when I dream, it's as if I am facing a dark glass; things aren't really clear. As I continue looking into that dark glass, it becomes an inner mirror, and I see the inside image of myself, the real me. I got a glimpse of the real me when I dreamed of hell. It was evident that I did not want to face what was going on inside me when I was awake. I ignored it, denied it, or was not aware of it.

Here's another example of the dark glass concept. One day I was shopping and looking, intensely looking, for a bargain in a department store. As I walked toward another rack of clothes, I saw a lady to my right and thought to myself, "That lady would certainly look better if she would just smile." I felt sorry for the lady because she looked sad.

Then reality hit. I had been walking by a mirror and, without realizing it, had seen my own reflection. I was that woman who looked so unhappy. I had no idea that was the image I was portraying. When I saw the real me, I didn't like what I saw. I realized that what I was supposed to have inside me (the joy of the Lord) was not showing on the outside. Shopping should never be that serious. I have never forgotten that experience and the depth of the feelings that rose up within me when I saw myself as others did.

Since then I have realized that a similar thing can happen to us in our dreams. We may not be consciously aware of some attitudes that need to be changed in us, but they can surface when we dream. As we look into the dark glass of our dreams, we get a glimpse of our real self, of what's really going on inside. When we awake, we can ignore the revelation or face it. We can react in a childish manner or respond as an adult (1 Corinthians 13:11). The choice is ours.

Then there are times in our dreams when the light comes on *behind* that mirror of dark glass, and the spirit realm bursts upon us as someone on the other side of the glass throws the switch. We then see beyond our inner selves and into the realm of the spirit. Though we may see or understand only in part, we still know we have had a glimpse of something, someone, or some place beyond this natural realm. Yes, our dreams can bring reality to us as we get brief views of that other dimension.

Don't discard the mirrors of your dreams! The Book of James tells us that when a man looks into a natural mirror, he beholds himself, walks away, and forgets what he has seen (James 1:23–24). But Paul tells us in 2 Corinthians 3:18 that "when we behold with open or unveiled face as in a glass the glory of the Lord, we are changed into that same image from glory to glory, even as by the Spirit of the Lord."

Responding to Your Dreams

Isaiah's response to seeing a vision of the Lord in the temple was, "I am a man of unclean lips."

Saul, a persecutor of Christians, fell beneath the brightness of a heavenly light and cried out, "Lord, what will you have me to do?"

When I had that dream of hell, I felt the same way as these men. "I am a woman with unclean motives," I told the Lord. "What do you want me to do?" I was compelled to make things right, and I did. Once you have seen or visited that other realm, you are never the same. The spirit realm is as real as this earthly realm, and through dreams and visions, it can be made known to us!

Maybe, like I was, you have been struggling over someone's personality or the methodology of other Christians, your mate, a friend, or even your pastor. I trust that the sharing of my dream of hell helps you to see *you*. If you know you've had a critical attitude toward someone, ask the Lord to forgive you. Remember that God can use other people's personalities and can use people in spite of their personalities.

Calling the Lost

Another awesome benefit of dreams is that they are also a part of God's plan of love to call out to the lost. I did not realize this until I got into this study. I don't think any of us can truly fathom the depth of God's love for all of us. The Bible lets us know that God so loved the world that He gave His only Son to die for us. That's real love. God sent His Son, His people who are witnesses of His love, His prophets, His evangelists, His pastors, His Word, and His Holy Spirit; these have been sent to reach all people with the truth that God doesn't want anyone to perish but wants all to have everlasting life.

If people continue to ignore His message and messengers, God can reach out to them while they sleep. Look at Job 33:14–18:

> For God speaketh once, yea twice,
> yet man perceiveth it not.
> In a dream, in a vision of the night,
> when deep sleep falleth upon men,
> in slumberings upon the bed;
> then he openeth the ears of men
> and sealeth their instruction,
> that he may withdraw man from his purpose
> and hide pride from man.
> He keepeth back his soul from the pit,
> and his life from perishing by the sword.

When I discovered this Scripture, I realized even more the far-reaching love of God. This verse reveals that through dreams and visions God opens the ears of man (not the ears attached to our head, but our spiritual ears of perception) in order to make Himself known. I believe the Lord will even give warning to those who love Him but have not been sensitive to hear Him. Even

Christians can become cold to the Lord. If we are not heeding His message of love when we are awake, God can come to us in our sleep and stir up our God consciousness.

As I continued to study Job 33, I began to notice that God speaks three times. To me this means that God touches the three dimensions of man: spirit, soul, and body. God speaks once when people physically hear the gospel message. Then if they do not respond, God will speak *twice*. This could be while people are in meditation, and their natural daydream becomes a vision. This Scripture goes on to say that if people yet do not perceive, then God comes a third time; this time He comes in a dream or night vision. It is then that God opens (makes plain, reveals, uncovers) the innermost perception of the third dimension of man, which is the spirit of man, in order to make Himself known. It seems that dreams are truly a tool of God's love.

I was so touched by the message of this Scripture that as a teacher I wanted to know more about the depth of its meaning. I began to do a word study in the Amplified Version of the Bible, in *Strong's Concordance,* and in my *Zodhiates' Hebrew-Greek Study Bible* to get further understanding. This study revealed that as we are in deep sleep, God can open our inner perception in order to seal instruction (warning, counsel against wrong practices, urge to duty) from Him; to withdraw us from our sinful desires (to take us in a new direction away from sin); and to hide (bypass) our prideful nature in order to reveal our heart's true condition; to keep us from the pit (of destruction) and our lives from perishing (prematurely) by the sword (violently). This shows me God wants us to fulfill our days and not be cut off from the life He has for us.

Then another revelation came to me. I began to realize that if I were witnessing to people who would not listen to me when they were awake, then I knew I could pray for them and over their sleep. Then God could deal with them through their dreams as they slept. I first found out that this works when I began to pray over our children's sleep.

Answering Prayer

When I realized that the Lord could minister to us in our sleep, I became so excited about what I was learning that I wanted everyone to know. I must admit that I did go a little overboard. At that time, our son, Jeff, was a teenager, and he was what we called "a Christian trying to backslide." We were praying for him and trying to walk him through this stage of his life. It was difficult to have family devotions because of the age difference between our oldest and youngest son (fourteen years difference). I think the enemy fights family unity more than he fights anything else. We would get into a time of devotion, and our youngest son, Jason, would ask if we could sing "Jesus Loves Me."

Jeff would make a face at him and whisper, "Shut up," and confusion would begin.

Fred or I would get upset and yell, "Would you quit that so we can have devotions! This is a time to be spiritual!" By that time, of course, the devotional time was ruined.

I eventually discovered that I could divide and conquer. I began to go to the bedroom of each of our four children and have prayer with them individually. Going to their rooms became a wonderful opportunity for them to open up and share things that they would not have shared in a group. The first night this new transition began, I went into Jeff's bedroom and asked if I could pray for him (not *with* him because I knew he wasn't praying at the time). He rolled his eyes and said, "Okay, Mom."

As I laid my hand on his head, he stiffened up. It was like praying for a corpse. But I prayed anyway, just a simple prayer. I prayed for the Lord's protection over him and for the Lord to reveal Himself as Jeff slept. I hugged him, told him I loved him, and left. I did this consistently with all four of our children for a long time.

During this time, Jeff was going through that teen stage in which he wanted to be a cool guy at school, so he decided he didn't want to go to church anymore. Usually, our children are in church whenever the doors are open because they are PKs (preacher's kids). When he declared that he wasn't going to church anymore, we told him he would go with us as long as he lived in our home. He then said he was leaving, and we said we would help him pack. He then backed down for a while. This same conversation took place often.

One day Jeff said, "Okay, I'll go to church, but on my terms." He meant he would dress the way he wanted to when he went to church. The first Sunday that he dressed how he wanted, I almost fell over when I saw him. The Lord helped me keep my mouth shut. Jeff thought he could embarrass us into saying he didn't have to go to church anymore, but it didn't work. It was now fall, and school had started; he dressed nice for school, but on Sundays he was a wrinkled mess. I don't know where he got those clothes. He sat in the back row of church and slid down in his seat until I couldn't see his head (and he was over six feet tall). People commented to us about his dress and his attitude, but we honestly didn't care. We knew a secret: "Faith cometh by hearing, and hearing by the word of

God" (Romans 10:17). While Jeff was coming to church, he was hearing the Word, and we knew the Lord could touch him.

Months went by, and school was over for the year; summer break began, and to our happy surprise we began to see a change in Jeff. That summer our church had an old-fashioned tent meeting on our church grounds, and before it began, the evangelist said that the meeting was going to be a time for the Lord to touch our youth. Jeff and Kim were in public high school at the time, and the revival was so powerful that they brought more than sixty-five of their schoolmates to the tent meeting that summer.

One night the evangelist called for young people to come forward to the altar. The altar was packed with teens; some were dressed in shorts, some were barefoot, some were saved, and some were not. The front was so crowded that the minister could not step down from the platform, so he stretched out his hand toward the teens and began to pray for them. Suddenly, the presence of the Lord filled that tent, and those young people began to fall under the power of the Holy Spirit. There were no catchers. Kids fell on chairs, on the poles of the tent, and on one another. No one was hurt, but I could hear some of them yell as they unexpectedly fell over. Some began weeping and praying; others just lay wide-eyed and shocked. Some tried to crawl back to their seats or out of the tent. The sight was amazing. It became a powerful youth revival, one that is still fondly remembered by those who were there.

A few days after the meeting, Jeff came into our bedroom as we were getting ready for bed. He flopped across our bed and casually said, "I don't know if you've noticed or not, but I've been making some changes in my life." (We had noticed but didn't want to make a big deal about it.)

He continued, "Well, Mom, remember when you first started coming in our rooms to pray for us? The first night you prayed that the Lord would reveal Himself to me in my sleep. I just laughed to myself. But that very night as I was sleeping I had a dream, and the Lord spoke to me and said, 'Jeff, I have called you.' Immediately, I woke up and sat straight up in my bed. I was shaking and sweating, and my room was filled with the presence of the Lord. I told the Lord that night if He would give me time to straighten some things out in my life, I would give my life to Him. He gave me that time, and I have gotten those things right. I've given my life to the Lord!"

Jeff, Fred, and I began to cry, shout, and hug. Jeff became a powerful witness during his last year of high school; he later attended Rhema Bible Training Center in Tulsa, Oklahoma, and today he is still serving the Lord and is a preacher of the gospel. A mother's prayer was answered through a dream!

No one can convince me that praying over my loved one's sleep is not effective. Every time I look at our son, Jeff, I think of the powerful work God has done in his life, and it began with a dream. I have learned from experience that the Lord can call the unsaved through dreams. When you pray over your unsaved friends' sleep, expect to hear about their "crazy" dream. That's your assurance that the Lord has begun to open up their inner man and reveal Himself through their dreams. Your responsibility to be a witness to people when they are awake is not eliminated, however.

In the first and second chapters of the Book of Romans, the apostle Paul shared that no one will have an excuse when he or she stands before God. God is no respecter of persons; even if people have not known the law, they will be judged by their conscience (heart). Can it be that we will be judged by what has been revealed to our mind and heart while we are awake and even while we are asleep? I've heard several missionaries testify that when they went to a remote village, the villagers had already had dreams or visions of that One, but they did not know His name. These true stories should give us confidence because we know that we are declaring the name of the One who has already been revealing Himself.

Many people have shared with me testimonies of God's dealing with a loved one in a dream. Prayer over dreams is a weapon against the enemy! The night may be called God's secret place, but it is not a secret for Christians who understand the purpose of the night. Many testify that this weapon works! If your mate is unsaved, wait until he or she is asleep (and you hear snoring); then lay your hand on your mate and ask God to reveal Himself. Then be ready to hear the dream! You'll know God is at work. Expect your mate to be saved!

Along with praying over your family members' sleep, share with them the practical importance of their dreams. Help them to become aware that the night is God's time to minister to them as they sleep, and let them know that the night does not have to be a fearful time.

Chapter 9

Dreams: A Part of the Last Day Outpouring

"And it shall come to pass in the last days,"
saith God, "I will pour out of my Spirit on all flesh:
and your sons and your daughters shall prophesy,
and your young men shall see visions,
and your old men shall dream dreams."

Acts 2:17

Because I come from a Pentecostal background and have been a Christian for more than fifty years, I can remember when being Pentecostal was not popular, and we didn't even know the word *charismatic*. We were the few on the wrong side of the tracks. I remember that people would peer into the windows of my church and make fun of us. But now it seems the Holy Spirit is being poured out across denominational lines and around the world, and there are many wonderful and even challenging new things that churches are experiencing.

Being Overcome with the Spirit

One of those experiences that may be a challenge for some to understand is what we call being "slain in the Spirit." Earlier I mentioned that teens fell under the power of the Spirit in the tent meeting. You may have never experienced this yourself, but perhaps you have been in a service or have seen television services in which people crumple to the floor when someone prays for them. I believe this is a genuine experience, but it can become faddish. I've prayed for numerous people who have been overwhelmed by the presence of the Lord and have fallen to the floor. I've had unbelievers who knew nothing of this experience come for prayer, and when I lightly touched them, they fell to the floor. I have seen the shocked expressions on their faces as they go down. Afterward, they share with me that their falling was a sign to them of God's reality and power.

There are some scriptural references about this experience. Second Chronicles 5 says that the priests could not stand because the glory of the Lord had filled the house of God. Acts 9 says that Saul fell to the ground when he encountered the presence of the Lord and the heavenly light. The soldiers who came to arrest Jesus in the garden went backward and fell to the ground when He said, "I am he" (John 18:6). They had come into His overwhelming presence!

One of the reasons I'm sharing about this experience is that there seems to be a connection between being overcome with the Spirit and the dream stage of REM (rapid eye movement). A few years ago, a Catholic priest who is a friend of mine became intrigued when he started having special services; he began praying for people and saw them fall to the floor. He had done a general study on dreams, so he understood the REM factor. When he began to observe those who were on the floor, he noticed that some went into the dream stage of REM. He then interviewed those who experienced REM to find out what was happening to them. He found that many of those who remained in meditation for a while had some type of an experience with the Lord. Some felt they had received direction or peace, and others felt they had received healing. Of those who did not experience REM, few sensed any change at the time.

I'm not trying to say that falling when prayed for is a sign of the last day move of the Holy Spirit. In fact, I do not believe that. I'm also not indicating that if you go down when prayed for and do not stay down on the floor for a while or go into REM that you will not receive anything from the Lord. I just want us to realize that there should be more to being overwhelmed with the Spirit than falling down and experiencing no change.

The Outpouring Mentioned in Joel and Acts (Joel 2:28; Acts 2:16–17)

Through my study of dreams, I feel I have come into a greater understanding of the results of the last day out-pouring of the Holy Spirit mentioned in the books of Joel and Acts. Most of the teaching I've heard about this move of the Spirit has emphasized the baptism in the Holy Spirit and prophecy. When Peter stood up on the day of Pentecost, he did share with the people about this wonderful Holy Spirit experience. He then went on to say that this experience, which was foretold by the prophet Joel, would result in the Holy Spirit's coming on men, women, and children and would result in prophecy, visions, and dreams. As I continued studying these verses, I began to realize that prophecy is only one-third of this last day Holy Spirit move; dreams and visions are the other two-thirds! Look at this expanded version of the apostle Peter's proclamation on the day of Pentecost (AMP), which is a word study from both the Hebrew and Greek.[45]

But (instead) this is (the beginning of)
what was spoken by the prophet Joel:
"And it shall come to pass in the last days
[afterwards, after preparation made, latter end]," God declares,
"I will pour out [bestow, gush out, and shed forth]
of my Spirit [breathe forth a blast of air from my own breath]
upon all mankind [human nature with its frailties—
physical and moral—and its passions]."

It seems logical to me that the "all" referred to in this verse would include the Christian and non-Christian. I believe that as you continue to read this verse you will see that all (all people) can be reached through God's three-fold spiritual cord plan of prophecy, visions, and dreams.

"And your sons and daughters
(children, even including grandchildren)
shall prophesy (divinely speaking under inspiration,
showing and making known one's thoughts,
foretell events, speaking or singing
by inspiration in prediction or simple discourse,
telling forth the divine counsels).

As you can see, this begins with sons and daughters, then goes on to refer to only the young and old men. Somehow the women were not included in the next section of this verse. I questioned why the women had been left out until I discovered that the Hebrew word for *men* here is *bachuwr,* which includes the female gender. God has not left the women out!

"Your young men (choice, selected, chosen,
acceptable, excellent, fresh, regenerated youth
[including the female gender])
shall see visions (they shall gaze externally
and internally see an inspired appearance
and discern clearly—physically or mentally.
This experience will be contemplated with pleasure
and not only seen, but may be prophesied.
They shall behold, look, see, and take heed.
Revelation will even come

as they are [going into or] coming out of sleep).
Your old men (aged, elders, and pastors
[including the female gender])
will be caused to dream
(to bind firmly upon their hearts something
seen in their sleep which may be prophesied).

My next question is about the age difference between a young man and an old man. I have discovered that in the Hebrew culture a person was considered old (or older) when he or she had lived for one generation (forty years). Then the person was considered old enough and responsible enough to give wisdom to the younger generation. I now know what category I am in. Then I wondered why the young see visions but the old dream dreams? The only conclusion I can come to is that it is easier for a younger person to accept change; therefore, young people can be spoken to through visions. Usually, older people are more set in their ways, and I think the Lord must have made them sleep (or wait until they are asleep) to get through to them. Now I don't know this for a fact; it is just a thought!

"And upon my servants
(bondsmen, slaves, laborers, deacons, worshippers)
and upon my handmaidens
(female slaves, servants, bondswomen,
deaconesses, my family relatives)
I will pour out (gush forth) in those days of my spirit
(breathe forth a blast of air from my own breath)
and they shall prophesy
(divinely speak under inspiration through speaking
or singing by inspiration in prediction or simple discourse,
telling forth divine counsels and predicting future events
pertaining especially to God's kingdom)."

The number one way that God reaches all, of course, is through the preaching of the Word, which can come through prophecy. If all don't listen, God may reach out with a vision. On the road to Damascus, Saul saw a vision that radically changed his life forever. Stephen had already preached to him. It seems the vision was necessary to transform Saul. If people don't listen to a vision or have not yet heard the gospel message, another avenue of reaching all may come through dreams. These verses again remind us of the depth of God's plan of love.

The Early Church (Acts 5; 8—12; 16; 18; 21; 23; 27)

The three-fold spiritual cord of prophecy, visions, and dreams was very much a part of the early church. Cities were turned right side up due to the signs and wonders that took place. Prophecy was prevalent, but the early church ministers saw visions and were moved by spiritual dreams as well.

The apostle Peter said, "This is that which was spoken by the prophet Joel," (Acts 2:16) and the New Testament church started out with the supernatural downpour of the Holy Spirit in the upper room. Three thousand people were saved the very first day! God then continued to guide this new church and its leaders supernaturally. Angels rescued Peter and then Paul and Silas from prison. Stephen saw the heavens open, where Jesus stood at the right hand of the Father. Saul was called through a supernatural vision. An angel came to Cornelius at the same time that Peter saw a vision. The prophet Agabus gave forth prophetic revelation. Paul received the Macedonian call and revelations through dreams and visions recorded in the Book of Acts. Visions and dreams revealed the supernatural even as the other gifts of the Spirit did. The Holy Spirit was truly being poured out, and the early church and the world were deeply impacted. And it is still affecting the world today, as people are sensitive to the Lord.

The Holy Spirit's Outpouring Today

There are many evidences that point to the fact that we are living in the last days. The Holy Spirit is being poured out in our day across denominational lines, and the gifts of the Holy Spirit are being restored to the body of Christ. Today, millions around the world have received Christ as a Savior and been baptized in the Holy Spirit. We are blessed to see this happening.

Because the worldwide move of God is taking place today, I believe now is also the time that greater revelation of the purpose of dreams and visions will come to the body of Christ. Do not ignore this three-fold spiritual cord due to a lack of understanding. God is no respecter of persons. He will do for us even as He has done for others. God has a plan whereby He can pour forth His Spirit upon all flesh, even though we have physical and moral frailties. He wants you and me to be in on this outpouring; after all, we are a part of "all."

If you are in a stressful situation right now, realize that you can receive answers from the Holy Spirit as He quickens your inner man when you are awake and when you are asleep. The Lord has not left you without hope. He has a divine plan in place so that you can know Him and the mysteries of His kingdom.

I encourage you to take time to pray each day, learning to walk and talk with the Lord. Lay any struggles before Him in confidence that He knows how to help you. Then rest in Him. Expect that sweet sleep. Jesus said the Holy Spirit will always be with us; therefore, we can be led by His Spirit during the day, some of our daydreams can become visions, and we can be refreshed by His presence through our dreams even as we sleep.

A Prayer for Sleep

Dear Heavenly Father,

Thank you for being with me as I've been awake. I now dedicate myself and my time of sleep to you, for I know you will be with me as I sleep. Search my motives and do within me those things that you know need to be done. Make your deposit within me. I lay before you the struggles of today, and I thank you for showing me knowledge and wisdom through my dreams that will help guide me. I believe you will reveal your ways to me during my sleep.

Thank you, Lord, for peaceful rest and sweet sleep, for a refreshing in the night, and for the revelation that comes from you. I believe I will awaken a better person than I am now as I recall the dreams you have given me.

In Jesus' name,

Amen

When you lie down, you shall not be afraid;
yes, you shall lie down, and your sleep shall be sweet.

Proverbs 3:24 (AMP)

Chapter 10

Understanding Visions

Where there is no vision, the people perish.

Proverbs 29:18

My main purpose for this book is to emphasize the importance of dreams, not visions. But as I studied about dreams, I could not get away from visions. I have found that dreams and visions go together. Both dreams and visions can give practical wisdom or reveal the spirit realm. I used to think of a spiritual vision only as seeing some type of inspired appearance, but I learned that not all spiritual visions reveal the spirit realm. As people are meditating, they can see themselves working through an impossible problem. When this happens, they have received divine wisdom through a vision. Some of the Scriptures I'll be sharing will give examples of this. When I speak of spiritual visions, some may cringe because they've heard the visions of people who were rather unstable. After being in the ministry for many years, I can understand that feeling. I've heard my share of visions. But the false visions do not subtract from the power of the genuine visions. Think of the old saying, "Don't throw the baby out with the bath water." Although some people may go overboard, be insincere, or falter when learning to flow in the Spirit, we cannot ignore genuine spiritual visions. There are more stories in the Bible about those who have experienced visions than about those who have had dreams. Though the word *vision* itself may not be used, there are more than one hundred recordings of angelic appearances or statements such as "I looked and saw" or "The Lord spoke" that are actually referring to visions.

Visions are very much a part of the Bible. When Joshua was getting ready to go into battle, he saw the captain of the Lord of Hosts. Ezekiel was praying over his nation Israel when he had a vision of the valley of dry bones. Daniel was in a lion's den when he saw an angel shut the lions' mouths. There are references to visions in the life of Jesus. Jesus told Nathaniel, "You will see the heavens open." At the baptism of Jesus, God spoke from heaven, and the Holy Spirit descended in the form of a dove. Angels ministered to Jesus while He was in the wilderness and during His struggle in prayer in the garden. When Jesus took His three disciples with Him to the mountain, they saw a vision of Moses and Elijah. After Jesus' resurrection, He appeared to many as He came from beyond. While being stoned, Stephen saw into the heavens, where Jesus stood on the right hand of God. As you read through the Bible, I trust you will become even more aware of how often visions were a part of many people's lives.

Some supernatural experiences are at times referred to as visions. I refer to them as supernatural manifestations. In a vision, you *see into* the spirit realm; in a supernatural manifestation, the spirit realm *steps out* into the natural realm or you "step into a vision", meaning you participate in the vision in some way. For example, in Genesis 18, angels ate the food that was prepared by Abraham and Sarah. The men of Sodom saw the angels that rescued Lot in Genesis 19, and an angel actually smote Peter's side to awaken him in Acts 12. These angels apparently stepped out of the spirit realm into the natural realm, and the people seemingly participated in the vision with the angels. I encourage you to evaluate these biblical accounts for yourself and come to your own conclusion (see Hebrews 13:2).

Visions can etch on your spirit and connect you to your destiny—you can't get away from their impact. I now realize that I have had more visions than I realized at first, but I didn't know to accept them as visions at the time. Please understand that there will always be people who go off the deep end. But when people receive truth about a subject, they have guidance, understanding, and balance.

Visions can come to adults, teens, and children. Sometimes children are more open to the spirit realm than adults because children have a simplistic faith in God, and they haven't had enough time to be programmed not to believe. I've witnessed children experiencing the presence of the Lord and heard the testimonies of those who saw visions. They were too young to know the scriptural details of some of the things they had seen, but their visions inspired their families and the church. Samuel was just a child when the Lord began speaking to him (1 Samuel 3:4). Some childhood experiences with the Lord stay with us and can even sustain us into adulthood. When I was only ten, I had a vision of my grandmother that I have never forgotten. This vision came during a hard time in my life; my grandmother had died, and I was heartbroken. I was told that she had gone to heaven, but I didn't really understand what heaven was.

One afternoon, as my family and I were praying together, I remember looking up, with tears streaming down my face, and seeing the ceiling opened; I could see my grandmother's face clearly and the heavenlies behind her. She was smiling at me. As I focused on her beautiful, peaceful smile, my grief began to lift. I was surprised by how young she looked. I became excited and began to laugh. My family asked me what was happening, and when I told them what I had seen, they knew it was a vision from the Lord. That vision gave me the peace and assurance I needed. It also gave me a revelation of that heavenly realm and of what people look like after they get to heaven!

When our son, Jason, was a young boy, he had a vision during the night of three huge angels standing in his room. He was so scared that he ran into my bedroom. He described the angels in depth. Fred and I tried to explain to him that this vision was good, and then we prayed with him. Needless to say, he slept in our room that night. A year later, after a revival service, we took an evangelist out to eat with our children. As we were talking, the evangelist looked at our son and said, "Jason, I see three large angels standing by you."

We were shocked. Jason started shaking; he looked over at me and said, "See, I told you I saw three angels." This vision was a confirmation to my husband, Jason, and me. We know that the Lord has His hand on our son and that Jason is protected by angels of the Lord.

Visions or Daydreams?

There are several Hebrew and Greek meanings in the Bible for visions. I was surprised to learn that visions were seen mentally for the most part; as people gazed outwardly, they saw inwardly (or mentally perceived) an inspired appearance. Though some visions were viewed inwardly, they had such an impact that some people became sick or were in the spirit realm for days. Daniel was a good example of this. Not every vision was an inward vision, of course; some were seen outwardly. As people were in prayer or in deep meditation, the spirit realm opened before them.

When you think about the word vision, you may think of the dictionary meaning, "an image in your mind produced by your imagination, to have foresight." I call the dictionary definition a common-sense vision or a daydream, and it is a natural and necessary part of our lives. Due to a lack of common-sense vision, people can perish, and their lives can come to nothing.

Look around you. Visualization has become big business today. In our society, visualization teaches that if people will see themselves as successful or healthy, it will come to pass. They live what they picture in their mind, the vision they have on the inside. Natural vision (visualization), if used properly, can be of benefit to you. Actually, it is a godly principle. There is a need for both common-sense and spiritual vision. A spiritual vision goes to a deeper level than a daydream does and, similar to spiritual dreams, reveals an aspect of the spirit realm.

The Bible gives both practical and spiritual insight about the mind and our imagination. It gives us wisdom about what we should think because what we meditate on affects our daydreams and can prepare us for spiritual visions. Our attitude, according to the Bible, affects our mind; therefore, we should have a joyful and thankful attitude. In other words, don't let your circumstances "blow your mind." Our mind can be renewed, and bad thought patterns can be reversed if we think on truth, honesty, justice, purity, and good reports. This potential for change should give us hope. We do not have to adapt our thoughts to the negativity of the world or have an exaggerated opinion of our own importance (see Romans 12:1–3; Philippians 4:7–8). Joshua was told that if he would continually meditate on and speak the Word then he would have success (Joshua 1:8). These principles will work for us today, too.

Natural Visions

I have concluded that there are three types of visions: natural visions, spiritual visions, and supernatural manifestations. Natural visions are what we commonly call daydreaming, which involves pictures that pass through our mind twenty-four hours a day. These visuals in our mind are produced by our imagination. We can daydream with our eyes open or closed, and the images can change according to our words or circumstances. Begin to meditate or just close your eyes, and pictures will naturally pass through your mind.

You can control your thought life. You can receive wisdom or knowledge while meditating or thinking through (or visualizing) your situation. People have become successful due to solutions that have come to them as they meditated. Of course, you can fill your mind with wrong information and perverted images, and your daydreams can become vain imaginations or fantasies with no value to you. Overall, though, visualization or meditation is not wrong and can be a blessing to you.

Biblical References to Vision

The first three scriptural references let you know the importance and impact of vision. We are told that without vision people can actually perish, or as they cast off restraint end up going backward because of no direction. When vision comes, it stirs us and takes us forward. It needs to be written out in order to bring clarity and help in setting goals or even in getting others to become involved. Vision, whether considered spiritual or natural, is an absolute necessity in our lives.

If we don't have natural vision such as personal goals for our lives, we simply continue in the cycle of a non-productive lifestyle. The same is true when we do not have spiritual vision. We go around the same spiritual mountain again and again. Prayer attunes us to the message and timing of vision. Look at this Scripture about the importance of vision:

> Where there is no vision
> (to see an inspired sight or appearance,
> behold, look, gaze upon, receive spiritual revelation,
> mentally perceive, an oracle, prophesy)
> the people perish
> (go back, come to naught, become nothing).
>
> Proverbs 29:18 (AMP)

The type of vision referred to here is for people of influence, and we all have influence in some way, whether we are leaders, fathers, mothers, or friends. Vision is not only seeing an inspired sight but also having forethought and wisdom. The revelation received from this type of vision can be personal or can be shared with others so that they also can receive wisdom that brings about change. People can perish by continuing wrong patterns due to lack of vision, direction, and boundaries. Vision takes people forward.

Certainly, we want inspirational vision, but sometimes we become spiritually tired and need new vision. When that tiredness sets in, we as people of influence also can begin to sense that those around us start to lack inspiration. But there is hope. There is a second part to this verse. It says, "But he that keepeth (continues to believe, contends for, and waits for) the law (precepts, principles, instruction of the Word), happy (blessed, prosperous, and going forward) is he" (Proverbs 29:18b KJV). What does this mean? It means keep on keeping on! Vision will come and begin to take you forward if you just don't quit!

> And the word of the LORD was precious
> [rare, costly, withdrawn] in those days;
> There was no open [frequent, compelling,
> pressing, urging, widely spread]
> vision [spiritual revelation, insight,
> oracle, prophesy, to gaze upon, behold,
> see an inspired appearance, mentally perceive].
>
> 1 Samuel 3:1b

The Word keeps godly vision from perishing. First Samuel 3 begins, "And the child Samuel ministered unto the LORD before Eli." This verse is almost a paradox. Samuel, a young child, was ministering to the Lord, but no one else was. In Samuel's day, the word of the Lord was rare, withdrawn, or held back because the spiritual leaders had no open, compelling vision of spiritual revelation. Evidently, they had been caught up in the mundane, day-to-day routine of life. A dictionary definition of open is "not shut or hidden, but providing an entrance into, to spread forth, to be open to view." Visions were not open, and there was no entrance into the spirit realm because the leaders were spiritually insensitive. These leaders were not seeking after God. The result was that the nation was filled with chaos and sin, and people's lives were destroyed because the word of the Lord was held back.

But God never leaves us without hope. In that day, the Lord did have a young boy by the name of Samuel who was open to hear the voice of the Lord. I believe the same is true today. The Lord still has those who are sensitive to Him so that open vision will not cease, and the people will not go backward but forward.

Write the Vision

Write the vision [a sight, revelation, oracle,
to perceive mentally, contemplate, prophesy],
and make it plain upon tables, that he may run
[carry it out, bring it forth hastily]
that readeth it
[encounters it, comes upon it, it calls out to].

Habakkuk 2:2

It is necessary for vision to be written so that it can be made plain, clear, and distinct. Then those who read it may know how to carry it out. People are drawn to people of vision. When vision is written, it brings unity so that purposes can be accomplished. I'm not speaking of spiritual vision only. Vision can be achieved in our lives, in the corporate world, or even in the home. If the vision is not clear, people do not know in which direction to go; confusion, frustration, criticism, and discouragement set in, and eventually people quit or leave. If a church lacks vision, the purposes of God seemingly get lost, and sometimes the pastors or leaders do not even understand what has happened. When we sense a vision for our life, we need to write it down, or it will lose its impact on us.

Spiritual Visions

Spiritual visions can come as they are inspired by God's spirit, as God speaks to our spirit, or as our spirit cries out to God. When you are in meditation or prayer, the Holy Spirit can open your inner man to see beyond natural daydreaming into the realm of the spirit, or you can receive divine wisdom and direction as you see yourself work through an impossible situation. Mini-visions can come as a flash of pictures to your mind. You may hear a voice or just see images. Spiritual visions bring wisdom or revelation from a realm beyond this natural realm, and they have been known to change lives, churches, and even nations.

Spiritual visions do not come simply because we wish for them. They are not something to be taken lightly. All images that pop into our head are not spiritual visions. Most are from our natural thinking. In the Bible, those who saw into the spirit realm, for the most part, were people who walked with the Lord. I want to assure you that I am not talking about the New Age concepts of meditation and visualization.

The Purpose of Visions

Visions and dreams have the same purpose, but visions take place during a time of consciousness, when our physical or spiritual ears and eyes are opened so that we're able to hear or see into the spirit world. You may have never thought about this, but I believe we have two sets of ears and eyes—physical and spiritual.

One example of this is the young boy Samuel. As he was ministering to the Lord, the Lord spoke to him in a night vision, "Behold, I will do a thing in Israel, at which both the ears of every one that heareth it shall tingle" (1 Samuel 3:11). I believe this verse reveals that because the word of the Lord was rare and there was no open vision or spiritual revelation during the time of Samuel, the physical and spiritual ears of the people had become dull and insensitive to the Lord's messengers and His message. But God was about to do something that would cause both the ears of the people to tingle or *to continue to ring with astonishment.*

You may ask, how does a person hear or see in a vision? I think the Hebrew meaning of *ears* in this verse gives us an indication that we are to have "pondering" or "giving-heed" ears, or you could say that we hear not only with the natural ears but also we are sensitive to hear with the inner ears (heart or inner perception). "Pondering" what is heard to the point that it is heard (and or seen) on the inside so that we "give heed" to change our actions. Because the child Samuel ministered to the Lord, he had heard not only with his physical ears, but also his spiritual ears. Seemingly, Eli did not hear the voice.

Acts 22:9 could be another example of being sensitive to hear in a vision. Paul testified that when he saw a vision of the light from heaven, he distinctly heard the Lord speak, but those with him did not hear the voice of Him that spoke to him; they only saw the light. In that vision, did he just hear physically? We know that seeing the vision and hearing the message that came through that vision changed his life. Job 33:14 begins with "For God speaketh once, yea twice, yet man perceiveth it not." It goes on to say that in a dream or *vision of the night . . .* then the Lord opens the ears (same reference of *ears* as 1 Samuel 3) of men, meaning the inner ears or perception of men, and seals their instruction. Jesus said in Matthew 13:11 that if the people were sensitive to *hear* the messages of His parables, they could not only know the mysteries of the kingdom of heaven, but be converted and healed. He went on to explain why they did not know; it was because their heart (inner man) was dull of understanding or hearing. Thankfully, Jesus didn't leave it there; He continued in verse 16: "But blessed are your eyes, for they see; and your ears, for they hear."

142

An example of both sets of eyes is found in 2 Kings 6. Elisha and his servant were surrounded by enemy forces, and the servant was in great fear. Elisha prayed that the Lord would open the eyes of this young man, and the young man saw the vision of horses and chariots of fire. His spiritual eyes had been opened.

The Scripture reveals to us a variety of situations in which visions were manifested. In the early church, they occurred during worship, prayer, fasting, times of seeking truth, and times of crisis. Visions came to men, women, and even children. Through visions, God gave His revelation to men and women and revealed His glory. Isaiah and Daniel saw into the spirit realm as if they were in a dream. Balaam, Peter, and Paul saw as if they were in a trance with their eyes open. Jeremiah saw when in deep meditation, and Daniel sometimes saw into the spirit realm when he was in prayer. On the other hand, some such as Ezekiel, Isaiah, Zacharias, Peter, James, John, and Ananias saw visions and had divine encounters during the course of their everyday duties.

The Results of Visions

Visions can accomplish many things. Men and women were encouraged, strengthened, and directed as God's Word was confirmed. Through visions, God's glory and power were revealed and changed the people who saw them. People became humble and were in awe of God after experiencing a vision. They were cleansed and readied to heed God's call. They received more compassion, a burden for the lost, and a burning desire to share God's love with others. Visions produced more results than merely spiritual goose bumps!

No matter whether a person was awake, meditative, or trance-like, God's message was always clear, awesome, and shaking. People knew a vision was from the Lord. If you have what you think is a spiritual vision but do not see a change in your life, I recommend you reevaluate the vision. Maybe you were just daydreaming.

The Impact of Visions Today

Although I believe God is still speaking to people through visions, I don't want to leave you with the impression that natural daydreams are not necessary, nor do I want to make you think that you will experience spiritual visions every day. The visions recorded in the Bible had a definite purpose for a specific time. I believe the same is true today; visions come for a definite purpose at a specific time. For example, Daniel had several visions that impacted him and his nation, but these visions did not happen on a daily basis. In fact, two of his visions were several years apart.

Visions can impact unbelievers. Recently, we had a lady share her testimony at our church. She is originally from Asia, and before she came to the United States, she knew nothing of Jesus. In her inspiring story, she told us that one day as she was leaving her temple, she looked up in the sky and cried out, "If there is really a God in heaven, show yourself to me."

As she continued to look up, she saw the appearance of a man with his arms outstretched across the sky. She was in awe as she saw blood dripping from his hands and feet. When the blood hit the ground, people would spring up out of the ground with their hands upraised.

144

The vision faded as quickly as it had come, but it did not fade from her heart. She had no idea what the vision meant. She began to tell others about her vision and asked them if they could help her, but no one knew what to tell her. She didn't know what to do, but she held on to the memory of that vision.

A few years later, she came to America. After being here a few months, a neighbor invited her to a Catholic church. She agreed to go. When she entered the church, the first thing she saw was the huge crucifix on the wall. "Who is that man?" she cried out.

"Why, that's Jesus," answered the neighbor.

With tears streaming down her face, she said, "Tell me about Him. He is the God I have been searching for." Today, she is a powerful Christian witness because of the impact of a vision.

A Vision: Two Men in Black and a Man in White

My grandfather had a vision when I was a child. My Grandpa Powell was a good, moral man and a hard worker, and I loved him dearly. When he was young, he had a vision of one of those old-fashioned scales, and he saw that one side was hanging low. A voice said, "You have been weighed in the balance and found wanting." This so shook him that he prayed and accepted the Lord. However, as time passed, the vision faded, and so did his walk with God.

As an older man, he was on his way home from work one day when he became gravely ill. While fighting the sickness, he had another vision. This time he saw a deep hole, and he sensed he was being forced into it. He knew it was hell, and he was terrified. That vision was a wake-up call from God, and Grandpa heard it. With his son, Bruce, who had recently become a Christian, he prayed to get right with God.

Despite his prayer, Grandpa still struggled with some of his old habits. Later that year, an illness forced him to stay in the hospital, and there he slipped into a coma. His family took turns staying with him. On New Year's Eve, while Bruce was on his way to the hospital to take his turn, he prayed, "Lord, I've got to know if things are right between You and Dad. Please allow him to come out of that coma so I can talk with him. If Dad is awake when I get to the hospital, I'll know you've heard me, and if you still want me to preach, I'll preach." (Bruce had been struggling with the call to be in ministry.)

When Bruce walked into his hospital room, Grandpa turned his head and said, "Hello, Bruce." Bruce fell to his knees beside the bed and asked, "Dad, is everything all right between you and the Lord?"

Grandpa replied, "I'm so afraid." Bruce could sense a terrible resisting presence in the room, and he began to cry out in prayer. He laid his hand on his dad and earnestly prayed for more than an hour.

Suddenly, the awesome presence of the Lord filled the room, and at the same time, the sounds of New Year's celebrations interrupted Bruce's praying; the sounds of firecrackers, horns, and shouts were heard.

"Dad," Bruce said, "the New Year has begun."

Grandpa replied, "Yes, and a new man, too."

They continued to talk for a while, and Grandpa explained what happened before Bruce arrived at the hospital that night: "I've always been afraid of death. Before you came into the room, two men in black were standing at the foot of my bed, and I was terrified. While you were praying, a man in white came and stood between me and the two men in black. The man in white said, 'You cannot have him. He belongs to me.' Then I heard the sounds of New Year's celebrations and realized that I had been made new, too."

A while later, Grandpa spoke again. "I see a beautiful city on a high green hill. Can you see that city, Bruce?"

"No, Dad," Bruce replied. "Only you can see that." The peace of God settled into my grandfather's heart, and that night his fear of death left. He lived several more months before going to be with the Lord. My Uncle Bruce became a youth pastor, and he is still a pastor forty-four years later!

How Can I Prepare for Visions?

I believe my grandfather had several visions because other people were praying for him. However, that does not always happen. Perhaps you have never experienced what you would call a spiritual vision, but you desire to be open to the Lord. The next step is to then have a consistent relationship with Him through prayer, His Word, and worship. You don't have to be perfect to get to know Him on a personal basis. Your relationship with the Lord will mature you and allow you to become sensitive to the reality of the spirit realm.

Life will lead us through many roads of testing. Often, we must walk by faith and not by sight. We may not feel or see the Lord, but we can know Him by faith. Even if we do not have supernatural experiences, our consistent walk of faith builds and deepens our relationship with the Lord and causes us to know that He is real and that the Bible is true. Along the way, however, there are times when the Lord can confirm His Word by allowing us to get a glimpse of the spirit realm.

Biblical Examples of Those Who Experienced Visions

The Bible makes us aware of many who had a consistent walk and relationship with God. Abraham went through many tests in his life, and he easily could have given up. But he had such a close relationship with the Lord that God called him friend. After starting his ministry at age eighty, Moses spent his last forty years with the murmuring Israelites. Yet God spoke to him face to face. Samuel, a prophet and seer, had a pure heart from the time he was a child. The prophets Isaiah, Jeremiah, Ezekiel, and Daniel did not allow their captivity to keep them from their relationship with God. In fact, they became witnesses to their captors.

People use various excuses for not living a Christian life. I encourage you to make up your mind to serve the Lord! Your age or gender should not be a factor that keeps you from having a relationship with the Lord. God sent the angel Gabriel to appear to Zechariah, an elderly man. Then Gabriel was sent to Mary, a young woman who had found favor with God (Luke 1).

Your past does not gauge the depth of the relationship you can have with the Lord. After experiencing a vision on the road to Damascus, Saul, a man who persecuted Christians, became Paul, a man who laid down his life for Jesus. In Acts 26:19, Paul, near the end of his life, shares before King Agrippa that he had not been disobedient to the heavenly vision. John and Peter, rough fishermen, became fishers of men and knew what it meant to follow Jesus and to see into the spirit realm. Women who had been forgiven by Jesus did not forsake Him after He died. They followed Him all the way to the tomb, where there was an angel to inform them that Jesus had risen!

The Bible says that those who had visions of importance had set their face to seek the Lord. Daniel sought the Lord through prayer and fasting with sackcloth and ashes, and while Daniel was praying and confessing his sins and the sins of the nation, he saw a vision. At another time, Daniel had been mourning and fasting for three weeks when he had a vision of the Messiah (Daniel 9:3–23; 10:2–21). Isaiah had come to the temple to pray and, no doubt, to mourn over the death of King Uzziah when he saw the King of kings high and lifted up with His train filling the temple (Isaiah 6:1).

In the Old Testament, men who saw visions were called *seers*. *Chozeh,* the Hebrew word for seer, means "a beholder in visions, a prophet, gazer, discerner, and one who perceives mentally and prophesies." For example, Zadok, the high priest under King David, served as a leader of music and worship (1 Chronicles 16:39–40 and 2 Samuel 15). Ananias was a New Testament seer; he was the disciple who was called to visit Saul, the persecutor who had been blinded by a vision on the road to Damascus (Acts 9:10). Agabus, another seer, prophesied the great famine and foretold that Paul would be bound in Rome (Acts 11:28; 21:10). Barnabas, Simeon, and Lucius were also prophets and seers (Acts 13:1). These men were godly and bold and had great influence in their day. These people make a varied group, yet the common thread in their supernatural experiences is that they had a consistent relationship with the Lord. Christianity is not about religion; it is about relationship!

Historical Examples of Visions

Visions have impacted people throughout history. George Washington saw a vision of the wars that would involve America and Europe. Joan of Arc saw a vision in which she was chosen to liberate France from the British. She believed in this vision, and at age seventeen she led the armies of King Charles VII of France into battle against the English in 1429. Lord Alfred Tennyson in 1842 saw a vision of airplanes and sky fighting. This vision came long before even the automobile was invented! Tommy Hicks, who conducted the great Argentine revival, was in Canada July 25, 1961, when he saw a vision of the rising of the great "sleeping giant," the body of Christ.

Visions Today

Because of this study, I've reflected on my life and realized that I have had more visions than I at first thought I had, but previous to this study, I didn't know to accept them as such. I have witnessed the cloud of glory settle into some of our church services. It appeared as a mist or fog. Usually, other people did not see the cloud but could sense the presence of the Lord. People have told me that they have seen angels surrounding our church auditorium. I did not see them. When people tell me that they saw a vision at my church, usually there has been an unusual presence of the Lord in the service. Sometimes I'm not sure there was an actual vision, but I leave that decision with the Lord and with the person.

There have been times during prayer when I have been overwhelmed by the presence of the Lord, but I did not actually see an inspired appearance. Other times I have had an inward witness or view as I've prayed for people. A few times I've had a mini-flash of pictures come to my mind, and I'm not sure if they were visions. I've been in prayer before speaking at a service and have had a person's face appear before me. I didn't know the person. Sometimes I receive a word to share, and other times I just continue to pray. Every time I've experienced this, the person whose face I saw has been at the service.

Not every vision is clear even though it may have a powerful effect. One vision that was both impacting and very different took place when Fred and I were in Bible college. We were just a couple of young Bible school students who were hungry for God. We were in one of our many decision-making times. We went to bed, but I could not sleep. So I prayed. We lived in a small house off campus, and it had a room that was too small to be a second bedroom; we called it our prayer room. When I went into that room and began to pray, I thought it would just be a typical prayer time. But as I began to call out to the Lord that night, I was overwhelmed by His presence.

As I was wiping the tears from my eyes, I saw a bright light hovering in the corner of the room. There was no form inside the light. The light seemed to move, but it did not take on a definite shape. I began to tremble, for I knew it was supernatural. The presence of the Lord became so heavy that I felt as if I could not breathe. I finally lay on the floor with my face buried in the small piece of carpet we had in the room, and I just continued to weep. I stayed for a long time, and His presence became even heavier. Eventually, I went to Fred, woke him up, and said, "Come with me. The Lord is in this room."

Fred was sleepy and had a puzzled look on his face, but he came with me. As soon as we entered the room, we both fell on our knees. The light was still there. The heavy presence of the Lord was still there. We were overwhelmed by His presence and His love. We spent most of the night in that room until the light began to fade. There was no voice, no defined image, but we certainly received the strength, encouragement, direction, and revelation of the Lord as we sat that night in His presence.

Hindrances to Visions

Certainly, Satan can imitate or pervert visions. There are cults that have been established on one person's vision. False visions can come when one attempts to establish ungodly principles or deception. Isaiah said that strong drink and drugs can cause a person to have false visions (Isaiah 28:7). People on LSD, cocaine, and all types of drugs have had terrible hallucinations.

Supernatural visions can come to unbelievers as well as to believers. The Bible describes a warning vision that came to King Belteshazzar, a man in drunken rebellion who saw the finger of God write on the wall of the palace (Daniel 5:5). The prophet Balaam had supernatural visions of warning, but his love of money caused him to sell out his own nation. The Bible says that Balaam's donkey saw a vision of an angel before Balaam did. Surely we can be more sensitive to the spirit realm than a donkey (Numbers 22:23).

Sin or a rebellious, unforgiving attitude will cause you to become spiritually dull and to close your spiritual eyes and ears. If you sense the need to ask the Lord to show you anything that may be hindering you from being open to the things of the Spirit, do that now. Then take the time to make a commitment to follow Him on a daily basis.

Prepare for the Results of Visions

After you are prepared to be open to spiritual visions, you need to prepare for what may happen to you when you do experience one. When Isaiah saw the Lord high and lifted up, the next thing he did was repent and say, "Here am I, send me." That vision changed the direction of Isaiah's life (Isaiah 6:1–8). Ezekiel is another man who responded to godly visions by repenting, and he was sent to the rebellious nation of Israel (Ezekiel 1). Visions, much like dreams, can be mirrors that reveal both the heavenly and our own inner spirit realm. Both Isaiah and Ezekiel experienced this. Daniel, a faithful man of God, was sick for days as a result of some of the visions he saw.

Is experiencing visions worth the cost of preparation? The apostle Paul had a phenomenal vision in which he was caught up to the third heaven. When he returned, the angel of Satan was waiting to buffet him for his revelation (2 Corinthians 12:1–6). The list of persecutions that Paul endured to follow Christ is in chapter 11. You would think that Paul would have been extremely discouraged, but just before he was martyred, he said with confidence:

For I am now ready to be offered,
und the time of my departure is at hand.
I have fought a good fight,
I have finished my course, I have kept the faith:
Henceforth there is laid up for me
a crown of righteousness,
which the Lord, the righteous judge,
shall give me at that day:
and not to me only,
but unto all them also that love his appearing.

2 Tim. 4:6–8

Regardless of how long we live here on this earth, there will come a time when we will lay this life down. What happens between birth and death is what counts. Visions can bring a reality to that realm beyond physical death. As pastors, my husband and I have been with people as they were getting ready to cross over to the other side. As the time drew near, we could tell they were more focused on that other realm than on this earthly one.

I trust that you will have an even greater desire to know Him, the Giver of visions and dreams. He wants you to know Him and the mysteries of the kingdom that He has to offer you. I am confident that as you walk with the Lord and have a consistent relationship with Him, He will make Himself known to you. Do not let anything or anyone steal that relationship from you. Remember Proverbs 29:18, which says that where there is no vision (spiritual revelations, insight, oracles which are prophesied), the people perish (go back, come to naught, become nothing). May God open both our eyes and ears! The spirit realm is real! God is real! My prayer for you is that you will have times in your life when you get a glimpse through that veil of dark glass into the spirit realm as you become aware of the purpose of the day, the night, your dreams, and your visions!

A List of Biblical Visions

The following list of Hebrew and Greek meanings for visions is for study purposes. This list does not cover all the visions of the Bible, but it will help give you a better understanding of the various visions and the way in which they were viewed. Please note that some of the Greek meanings for visions in the New Testament seem to be more descriptive than the Hebrew meanings of those of the Old Testament. I feel that some of these visions also could be supernatural manifestations.

Old Testament Visions

Chazah visions: to gaze and inwardly, mentally perceive; to contemplate with pleasure; behold; look; prophesy.

- Abraham: He had a *chazah* vision that confirmed God's covenant (Genesis 15:1).
- Balaam: Through a *chazah,* God verified His blessings on Israel and told Balaam to bless, not curse, Israel (Numbers 24:4).
- Daniel: He had several *chazah* visions as he was in prayerful meditation (Daniel 2:19; 8:2).
- Ezekiel: He prophesied against the prophets of Israel who saw vain *chazah* visions (Ezekiel 13:7).

Mareh **visions: seeing an appearance or mirror images, not a mental vision.**

- Aaron, Miriam, Moses: God told them that He makes Himself known to men through *mareh* visions (Numbers 12:6).
- Samuel: The Lord called to the child Samuel through a *mareh* vision (1 Samuel 3:15).
- Ezekiel: He was a prophet who had many *marehs* in which he saw divine appearances (Ezekiel 1:1; 8:3–4; 11:24; 37:1; 40:2; 43:3).
- Daniel: The angel Gabriel appeared to Daniel in a *mareh* (Daniel 8:16).

Chazown **visions: revelation of future events or something to come in a dream-like vision.**

- Job: He had *chazown* revelations that came in the night and caused both reverence and great fear (Job 4:13; 7:14).
- Job 33:15 says that God calls the lost through dreams and *chazown* visions of the night.
- Jerusalem was referred to as the valley of *chazowns* because so many men had visions there (Isaiah 22:1, 5).
- Isaiah: He was a prophet who saw grievous *chazown* visions of judgment to come (Isaiah 21:2).
- Ezekiel: He warned that there can be false *chazowns* (Ezekiel 13:16).
- Daniel: He had understanding in all *chazown* visions (Daniel 1:17; 7:1–28).
- See also 1 Samuel 3:1–2; 2 Samuel 7:17; 2 Chronicles 32:32; Psalm 89:19; Nahum 1:1; Habakkuk 2:2; Obadiah 1:1; Isaiah 1:1.

New Testament Visions

Optasia visions: to gaze with wide-open eyes at something remarkable.

- Zechariah: He was a priest who had an encounter with the angel Gabriel through an *optasia* (Luke 1:22).
- Women: They came to the tomb of Jesus and saw an *optasia* of two angels (Luke 24:23).
- Paul: He was caught up into the third heaven through an *optasia* (2 Corinthians 12:1–10).

Opaya-Horama visions: to gaze at, to discern clearly, and to experience.

- Jesus: He referred to the experience on the Mount of Transfiguration as an *opaya-horama* (Matthew 17:9).
- Saul: He experienced an *opaya-horama* of blinding, heavenly light (Acts 9:3).
- Ananias: while in prayer, he had an *opaya-horama* in which the Lord told him to go see Saul (Acts 9:10).
- Cornelius: He was an Italian soldier who was in prayer when he had an *opaya-horama* of an angel (Acts 10:3).
- Peter: while in prayer, he had a vision that revealed his prejudice (Acts 10:17).
- Peter: He was rescued from prison by an angel and thought he had seen an *opaya-horama* (Acts 12:7, 9).
- Paul: He had several *opaya-horama*, experiential visions that impacted his life (Acts 16:9; 18:9; 26:19).

Harasis **visions: to gaze in awe at an inspired appearance.**

- Peter: He shared on the day of Pentecost that the last day Holy Spirit outpouring would result in *harasis* visions (Acts 2:17).
- John: He was called the revelator because he had *harasis* visions of the Messiah and the future heaven (Revelation 1:10; 9:17).

Conclusion

Frequently Asked Questions about Dreams and Visions

This summary presents a brief overview of dreams, visions, and the purpose of the night. I want to highlight some of the important facts in order for you to have a quick reference.

Are dreams and visions God's will and plan?

God put the natural dreaming process in all people. He also placed within us the ability to visualize, creating an avenue whereby God can bring forth spiritual dreams and visions. Through dreams and visions, God's will can be revealed (see John 16:7–15). (See chapters 1; 2.)

What is the difference between a dream and a vision?

According to Acts 2:17–18, dreams and visions come to all. Dreams are our inner mind at work in us while we sleep. Dreams come from your inner man and are a series of symbolic pictures or stories or night parables that can convey principles for life. Visions are similar to dreams, but they come during a time that you are awake. Night visions can happen as you are either going into or coming out of sleep. (See chapters 1; 9; 10.)

How does God reveal Himself to us?

Through visions, God can make Himself known to us, and He can speak to us through the dark speeches of dreams (Numbers 12:6). Due to God's love for us, He will even make Himself known to unbelievers through dreams and visions (Job 33:14–18). The Bible says that the spirit realm can be revealed to us through the dreaming process because we are created in the image of God, and because we are spirit beings, we are connected to the spirit realm. We become God-conscious through dreams. Due to this spiritual revelation, we cannot deny the spirit world, and we will be without excuse when we stand before God (Romans 1—2). The last day outpouring of the Holy Spirit that is to come upon all flesh will come through prophecy, dreams, and visions (Joel 2:28; Acts 2:17–18). (See chapters 6; 9; 10.)

What are the dark speeches of the night?

Dreams are referred to as dark speeches, dark sayings, dark sentences, and parables of the night. Dark speeches refer to a type of riddle. The symbols of dreams must be discerned. Dreams are like the parables of Jesus because both dreams and parables are symbolic stories that speak to people's hearts and reveal spiritual mysteries (see Psalms 19:2; 49:4; 78:2; Numbers 12:8; Proverbs 1:6; Daniel 8:23; Matthew 13:34–35). (See chapter 6.)

Is natural dreaming a necessary process of life?

Dream experts have concluded that nightly natural dreaming is necessary for the good emotional and physical health of people. Dreams deal with the current situations of our lives. Because people work through their problems in their dreams, dreams are a God-given release from the stress of the day. Dreams are for you because they come from you. The Bible confirms that there are natural dreams (Ecclesiastes 5:3, 5:7; Job 7:14; Isaiah 29:7–8; Zechariah 10:2). (See chapters 1; 4; 5.)

What is the purpose of natural and spiritual dreams?

Dreams can counsel, give warning, impart knowledge, and bring solutions to seemingly impossible problems. While you sleep, your true motives can be made known, and blind spots in your life can be corrected. By dreaming, a person can be shown future events, can be taken into the spirit realm, can fight spiritual battles, and can see the power and glory of the Lord. Individuals and even nations have been affected by dreams. Do not ignore your dreams! (See chapters 5; 7.)

Aren't visions just daydreams?

Natural or common visions are considered daydreams, the images that come from our own imagination. In reality, images pass through our minds twenty-four hours a day. Wisdom can come as a person thinks through and visualizes a situation. But there are spiritual visions, too; these are not daydreams. Spiritual visions can be seen while people are in prayer or in meditation. People may be gazing outwardly but inwardly see an inspired appearance. The daydream becomes a vision as the inner man opens up to see into the spirit world (Proverbs 29:18; Daniel 2, 3, 5, 7; Isaiah 6:1; Numbers 22:23; Luke 1—2; Acts 10—12; and Hebrews 13:2). (See chapter 10.)

Do our dreams and visions need to be discerned?

You need to evaluate the messages of your dreams and visions to see what is being revealed to you. Also discern whether they are natural or spiritual. Determine whether the images are from your own imagination or from the Spirit. If someone else is the main attraction in your dream, discern if the dream is for that person. Remember that ninety-five percent of all dreams are for the person who had the dream, even if another person is featured. (See chapters 5; 7; 10.)

What is the real purpose of the night?

Read the following Scriptures, which share some wonderful aspects of the night.

- God's secret place (Psalms 18:11 and 81:7)
- A time God makes Himself known (Numbers 12:6–7)
- Inner self gives instructions (Psalm 16:7)
- Testing our hearts (Psalm 17:3)
- Spiritual songs (Psalm 42:8, 77:6; Job 35:10)
- Knowledge revealed (Psalm 19:2)
- Wisdom imparted (1 Kings 3:5)
- Secrets made known (Daniel 2:19–22)
- Calling the lost (Job 33:14–18)
- Sweet sleep (Proverbs 3:24)

Was the night created for good?

God created the night and said it was good. Dreams in the night revealed the future to Joseph, Pharaoh, the butler, the baker, Jacob, Peter, Paul, and many others. God spoke to men in the night through dreams and visions, and He gave direction and correction by opening the spirit realm. Solomon was gifted with wisdom, secrets were revealed to Daniel, angels appeared to the shepherds, and Paul heard the call to Macedonia. We are commanded by God to meditate on the Word day and night. Jesus knew the results of praying all night. The coming of the Lord will be as a thief in the night (Genesis 1:18, 37:5, 40:5, 41:1, and 46:2; 1 Kings 3:5; Daniel 2; Job 33; Luke 2:8, 6:12; Acts 16:9, 23:11; 2 Peter 3:10; and 1 Thessalonians 5:2). (See chapters 1; 6.)

No one hides in the night.

Jeremiah said, "Can any hide himself in secret places that God cannot see him?"

Daniel said, "God knoweth what is in the darkness and reveals deep and secret things." Jesus said of parables that they utter things that have been kept secret from the foundation of the world. If we will not listen to the voice of the Lord when awake, He will open our spiritual ears and make Himself known in the night while we sleep. Isaiah said that the Lord will give us treasures in darkness and hidden riches in secret places (Jeremiah 23:24; Daniel 2:19–22; Matthew 13:34–35; Job 33:14–18; and Isaiah 45:3). (See chapter 6.)

What are dreams anyway?

Dreams are images or symbolic stories that surface in your mind as you sleep. Dreams can be natural or spiritual, and both originate in your spirit man. During sleep, your inner man sorts through the circumstances of the day and quickens your brain to bring forth pictures to help give guidance. These pictures catch your attention and need to be evaluated because they are a vital part of your life; after all, dreams come from you! In spiritual dreams, the Holy Spirit intervenes in your dreaming process to bring divine wisdom or to open your inner man so that you see into the spirit realm. (See chapters 5; 6; 7.)

Does everyone dream every night?

Experts who have observed people's sleeping in sleep labs say that people dream every night. People dream for one to two hours each night and have approximately four to six dreams, which average fifteen to twenty minutes each. (See chapter 5.)

What happens when we sleep?

There are three stages of sleep: shallow sleep, dreaming, and deep sleep. These stages repeat themselves throughout the night. Children, even infants, have these same sleep patterns. During sleep, our spirit man evaluates our day's activities; the brain then brings forth pictorial parables in the form of dreams, which help us in working through various problems. (See chapter 5.)

How do you know a person is dreaming?

Scientists have measured dreams by attaching electrodes to the sleeping person's brain. During sleep, the brain is active and releases electrodes that can be electronically measured. The simpler way to measure dreams is to watch a dreamer's eyes move while they watch the pictures of the dream. This movement is called rapid eye movement (REM). Experts say that the brain never stops passing series of images through our minds. Generally, we do not pick up these pictures when we are awake because our minds are occupied with other thoughts. (See chapter 5.)

Can dreams be hindered?

Worry can cause insomnia, and the dreaming process can be hindered. An anxious person may even have a difficult time evaluating a remembered dream. There are other hindrances to sleep and dreaming, such as the continued use of alcohol or drugs. (See chapter 5.)

Does the Bible talk about dreams?

Actually, the Bible and science agree on the importance of dreams. Natural dreams, according to the Bible and science, come as a result of the business of life. There are thirty-four specific accounts of biblical dreams, twenty-two in the Old Testament and twelve in the New Testament. In reality, over one-third of the Bible refers to dreams, visions, and the purpose of the night. (See chapters 2; 4; 6.)

If dreams are so important, why is it so difficult to remember them?

Most important, our cultural teaching has given us the impression that dreams are not important. Other reasons include loud alarm clocks that can jar a dream from the memory. If you do not write down your dream, you will forget it. There also can be evil spiritual forces at work to keep you from remembering your dream so that God stays out of your life. (See chapter 7.)

Why can't I understand my dreams?

Dreams are symbolic—your inner man at work in you. These symbols are called the language of the Spirit. You may not know how to evaluate your dreams due to the symbols. You may not consider dreams to be important enough to take the time to think about your dream. You may not want to face yourself, the real you. Or you may not want to face God. (See chapter 7.)

How can I prepare to remember my dreams?

First, realize that you do dream every night. Get proper sleep. Then you must be ready to remember your dreams when you awake. Desire to hear through dreams. Cast down any vain imaginations or social or church traditions that may hinder your evaluation or cause you to think that your dreams are not important. Recognize that dreams will give knowledge and principles about your current situation.

As an act of faith, put a pen and a pad of paper next to your bed so that you can write down the dreams you remember. Awake to soft music as you meditate on what you were thinking as you awoke. When a dream comes back to your memory, take the time to write it down. Then evaluate your dream! Expect to receive help from your dreams! (See chapters 1; 7.)

How do I interpret my dreams?

Remember three words: simple, honest, and personal. Use your common sense. Learn the meanings of basic dream symbols. They will help you evaluate your dreams. When you remember a dream, look at it objectively to decide if it is natural or spiritual. Ask common-sense questions about the symbols of your dream, and relate your dream to your current situation. Your dreams should be biblically and principally sound. Do not strain to get the message of your dream. Remember that God wants you to know the meaning. As you think about the dream, be sensitive to the feelings you have on the inside. If you don't understand your dream, ask a godly friend to help you. (See chapter 7.)

How do I know if my dream is for someone else?

Although another person may be featured in your dream, the dream still may be just for you. It may be revealing your feelings toward that person or revealing that you should help the person in some way. If you come to the conclusion that the dream was for someone else, pray for guidance about whether or not to reveal the dream to the person. If you feel you should share the dream, pray about *when* and *how.* Whenever you do share a dream, leave people room to say whether or not the dream is for them. Do not take it personally if they say the dream is not for them. (See chapter 7.)

Can I learn to interpret other people's dreams?

Experts tell us we can learn to interpret others' dreams by first learning to interpret our own. Some experts say learning to interpret dreams takes at least five years. If someone asks you to help interpret a dream, become a coach by sharing the meanings of dream symbols. Never impose your own interpretation on other people. If you don't have any idea what their dream means, be honest.

They may need to pray and evaluate their dream further for themselves, and it may be for their ears only. (See chapter 7.)

Never attempt hasty interpretations of dreams by telephone or letter. You need an intimate knowledge of the dreamer's life before giving interpretations. If you feel God has blessed you with the ability to understand dreams, remember that the interpretation belongs to God and that only He can give you the wisdom to interpret dreams.

Are dreams and visions of value to me today?

Dream experts say that dreams are absolutely vital to the emotional, psychological, physical, and spiritual health of our lives. Dreams are free counselors that can help you face yourself and help you work through your day-to-day situations. Dreams are also an avenue by which God can minister to our inner man. Dreams give direction and correction, and they can show you what will happen if you continue on your current path. They also can reveal future events, help with spiritual warfare, and take you into the spirit realm. You may not have dreams for other people or prophetic dreams for the church, but all your dreams, natural or spiritual, should edify you. (See chapters 1; 5; 6.)

The Bible confirms the value of visions. Society is emphasizing the importance of visualization. Through visualizing, people have worked through their problems, have received wisdom, and have become successful. Through spiritual visions, divine revelation and wisdom can be revealed. Let's allow God to continue to work in us through both our natural and spiritual dreams and visions! (See chapter 10.)

Other helpful information can be found in:

- The Dream Survey (chapter 5)
- The List of Biblical Dreams (chapter 6)
- The List of Dream Symbols (chapter 7)
- The List of Hebrew and Greek Meanings of Biblical Visions (chapter 10)

NOTES

1. Winter, Ruth, "The Book of Dreams and Nightmares," *Ladies' Home Journal* (1989) 93–96, 99–101.
2. Helm, Mark, "Americans Need to Get More Sleep," *Dayton Daily News,* March 29, 1998.
3. Ward, Sam, "Are You Getting a Good Night's Sleep?" *USA Today,* March 27, 2000.
4. Riffel, Herman, *Your Dreams: God's Neglected Gift* (Lincoln, VA: Chosen Books, 1985).
5. Sanford, John A., *Dreams: God's Forgotten Language* (New York: J. B. Lippincott Company, 1968).
6. Riffel, ibid.
7. Winter, ibid.
8. Winter, ibid.
9. Jung, Carl G., *Man and His Symbols* (New York: Dell Publishing Co., Inc., 1968).
10. Strong, James, *New Strong's Exhaustive Concordance of the Bible* (Nashville: Thomas Nelson Publishers, 1990).
11. Winter, ibid.
12. Moss, Robert, "What Your Dreams Can Tell You," *Parade,* January 1994.
13. Riffel, ibid.
14. Moss, ibid.
15. Moss, ibid.
16. Lindskoog, Kathryn. "Dreams: Gifts in the Night," *Equipping the Saints Magazine,* Ministries International, Anaheim, CA, Volume 1, Number 6, November/December 1987.
17. Cartwright, Rosalind, *Night Life.* (New Jersey: Prentice-Hall 1977).
18. Winter, ibid.
19. Riffel, ibid.
20. Riffel, ibid.
21. Hurovitz, C., Dunn, S., Domhoff, G. W., & Fiss, H. "The dreams of blind men and women: A replication and extension of previous findings." *Dreaming,* 9 (1999) 183–193. The paper is available online at http://psych.ucsc.edu/dreams/Library/hurovitz_1999a.html (Accessed September 21, 2006).

22. Jung, ibid.
23. Winter, ibid.
24. Winter, ibid.
25. Kelsey, Morton T., *Dreams: The Dark Speech of the Spirit.*
    (New York: Doubleday Company, 1968).
26. Winter, ibid.
27. Riffel, ibid.
28. Riffel, ibid.
29. Winter, ibid.
30. Winter, ibid.
31. Morris, Jill, Ph.D., "Your Dreams: What You Can Learn from
    Them." *Good Housekeeping* (1987), 12–16.
32. Louersen, Neils, M.D., "Those Roller-coaster Feelings,"
    Expecting, Spring 1988.
33. Janiewicz, Debbie, "Sweet Dreams: Modern Solutions for
    Better Sleep," *Dayton Daily News,* November 5, 1998.
34. Moss, ibid.
35. Riffel, ibid.
36. Riffel, ibid.
37. Moss, ibid.
38. Brown, David Jay, "Unlocking the Secrets of Mind-Body
    Medicine: An Interview with Dr. Bernie Siegel. (Petaluma,
    CA: Smart Publications, Health & Wellness Update Magazine)
    June 2006. Available online at http://www.smart-
    publications.com/articles/MOM-siegel.php (Accessed Septem-
    ber 21, 2006).
39. Moss, ibid.
40. Morris, ibid.
41. Morris, ibid.
42. Riffle, ibid.
43. Riffle, ibid.
44. Riffle, ibid.
45. Strong, ibid.

About the Author

Katrina J. Wilson serves with her husband, Dr. C. Frederick Wilson, as co-pastor of Christ Life Church in Kettering, Ohio, an interdenominational, interracial church they founded in 1977. Katrina is an ordained minister with Calvary Ministries International and a graduate of Christian Life School of Theology.

Known as a dynamic yet practical and humorous speaker, Katrina travels nationally and internationally, speaking at churches, seminars, conferences, and women's retreats about victorious Christian living. She has been a Christian since childhood, is a devoted wife, a loving mother of four, and a proud grandmother of six.

Due to her in-depth study on dreams, this subject has become one of her most requested teachings. The need for balanced teaching on the largely misunderstood subject of dreams caused Katrina to put her years of study in writing. She also has written a study guide and has a six-tape series entitled "Understanding and Interpreting Your Dreams in the Night."

To order additional books, study guides, or audiotapes, write to:

Christ Life Church
4555 Marshall Road
Kettering, OH 45429

(937) 435-9055 or (937) 435-8814
office@ChristLifeNow.com
www.ChristLifeNow.com